Section Three

Your Website

Chapter 18
Do You Need an Expensive Website?

Chapter 19
What's In a Name?

Chapter 20
Which URL? Which is a Great URL?

Chapter 21
The Importance of Good Ancestors (& History)

Chapter 22
Don't be Two-Faced!

Chapter 23
Straplines and Your USP

I0507156

Chapter 24
Building an Online Family Tree

Chapter 25
Key Website Functionality

Chapter 26
No Cheating

Chapter 27
The Importance of Uniqueness and Good Content

Chapter 28
The Basics (Meta, images, content)

Chapter 29
Remember to be Sales Focused

Chapter 30
Being Sociable – Even If You Hate It

Section Four

Be Sociable – Even If You Hate It

A Bite-Sized Business Book

The Complete Practical Digital Marketeer

Your Guide to Digital Marketing Success

Stuart Haining ACIB, MCIM

Published by Bite-Sized Books Ltd 2018

Bite-Sized Books Ltd Cleeve Croft, Cleeve Road, Goring RG8 9BJ UK
information@bite-sizedbooks.com
Registered in the UK. Company Registration No: 9395379

ISBN: 9781729148433

Published by:

Bite-Sized Books Ltd
Cleeve Croft, Cleeve Road, Goring RG8 9BJ UK
information@bite-sizedbooks.com
Registered in the UK. Company Registration No: 9395379

To Ali & Viki

One who is cash rich (mostly with our money) but fritters
away her time, the other who suspects she could do
better with her money, but has no time!

Contents

Section One

Digital Marketing Is It Worth it – and Your First Steps

Section Two
Planning for Success

Chapter 9
Understand Your Numbers & Keywords

Chapter 10
Identify Positive & Negative Online Trends

Chapter 11
Research your Competitors

Chapter 12
Beware Search Engine Data

Chapter 13
Lifetime Value – Repeat Sales vs One Trick Ponies

Chapter 14
Online Budget Setting & Quick Tools

Chapter 15
Good vs Bad Savings

Chapter 16
Think BIG?

Chapter 17
Your Website

Section Five
Your On-Going Digital Marketing

Bite-Sized Business Books

Bite-Sized Books Catalogue

Foreword

by Professor Malcolm McDonald MA(Oxon) MSc PhD DLitt DSc.

As Sir James Dewar, the Scottish physicist said: "Minds are like parachutes. They only function when they are open." The reason I am quoting the great man is because I had become accustomed to viewing Stuart Haining as a great and hugely talented expert in the world of IT, particularly in Internet Marketing. I have worked with him over many years and he is not only brilliant at his area of expertise, but he is also a great raconteur and wonderful company. But did I ever see him as an author?

Of course not, hence my quotation above.

My mind was even more tightly closed when I got wind of his intention to write a book about Online Marketing.

As Bill Bryson said in The Road to Little Dribbling: "The thing about the Internet is that it is just an accumulation of digital information, with no brains and no feelings--- just like an IT person!" So it was with some trepidation that I opened this book by Stuart about Online Marketing. I quickly discovered, however, that Sir James Dewar was correct and I felt duly chastened on reading this little book. Bill Bryson, on the other hand, was totally wrong in his reference to IT people. What I found remarkable was the way Stuart has converted his expertise and wisdom into what is a pleasant, witty (and at times a little cheeky) book. Unlike most books, this one is entertaining as well as being hugely useful and practical.

I have written and published forty five books, but I will now see if I can persuade Stuart to abandon his consultancy work and re-write all my books in his own, inimitable style.

Professor Malcom MacDonald

Professor McDonald enjoys a global reputation as a leading authority on Marketing. He was until recently Professor of Marketing and Deputy Director at Cranfield University School of Management, and is now an Emeritus Professor at the University as well as being an Honorary Professor at Warwick Business School. He has been consultant to many major companies in the areas of strategic marketing and marketing planning, market segmentation, key account management, international marketing and marketing accountability. Malcolm is Chairman of six companies and works with the boards of some of the world's leading multinationals. He has written over 40 books including the best-selling Marketing Plans: How to prepare them, how to use them and Marketing Accountability.

Introduction

Online Marketing, Panacea or Pain in the ....?
Aka, Tricks of the Trade

Thank you for purchasing this book which covers the whole range of digital marketing, I hope you find it useful in ways you hadn't expected plus the ones you'd hoped for!

I don't know if you'd agree with the familiar sentiment that *everyone has a book inside of them* (or perhaps share my view *I wished they'd kept that book to themselves*!)? Either way, we have our mutual friends at Bite-Sized Books to blame for this journey through the exciting foot-hills of marketing online and internet trading!

I confess I would have been happy for the contents, to have stayed my secret, tricks of the trade learned over 22 years in online marketing which are only normally revealed under duress as occasional snippets to our fee-paying consultancy clients. But Bite-Sized know better and assured us there is a huge, yes, they said *huge*, eager audience crying out for such pearls of wisdom!

With that encouragement we've set out to share tips about pitfalls and shortcuts learned at the e-commerce coal-face. Blame them if it's not up to the Dickens or Wodehouse standard you'd hoped for and you get a mix of my individual views or the team's back at the coal-face!

At the very least, the contents should be a little different from your everyday marketing books (and many good ones get into the detail of how to *DO* Online Marketing but few share tricks and pitfalls) and all the usual stuff available to marketing and business students. Enjoy.

Stuart Haining

Northampton, England

Section One
Digital Marketing

Chapter 1
What is Marketing? Do you really need it?

Most businesses or organisations, even one-man-bands, are going to need to carry out some level of marketing to generate sales leads or help to create an initial list of prospects. From that they can then start to communicate regularly via the myriad of channels now available and accessed eagerly by their unwitting recipients. Creating these communications is a time consuming and potentially expensive process but all being well should create a lead generation pipeline which starts off the sales cycle, if sales transactions are what is desired. Or if preferred it could lead to sign-ups, followers, membership or some other form of brand adulation.

But the world is changing fast. All the aforementioned media are starting to overload the poor consumer or business person. In general people are starting to become even more selective. We and pick and choose more than ever before how, when and where we will give away our time to be marketed to. Be that in simple browsing, absorbing the message or actually responding. Added to this is the complication that increasingly it's not uncommon for prospects to *touch* an organisation multiple times across several channels before making any decision to do anything, which of course makes it very hard to track real cause and effect.

Hopefully this paints the start of a picture explaining why even the smallest error in planning your Marketing strategy and or the precise elements of your advertising mix can be costly, both in time and money.

It's probably a good idea then for this book to try and save you some hassle and see if you might actually ignore marketing altogether?

It's unusual, but if you can crack this trick it's a huge boost for any fledgling business or new project, and sometimes government intervention and rules will cover almost all the heavy lifting (and cost) for you!

OK, so how to decide?

First off, its vital to think through in advance precisely what you need to achieve and not just trust to luck, falling back on the same old marketing you see everyone else doing. Your organisation's marketing needs to have the highest possible relevance to its planned audience, so off-the-shelf methodology may be great when buying a new shirt or blouse, it's rarely good when considering a marketing strategy as you need to stand out.

Few people start a business straight from school or university, they will have gained a few years' experience working for other people, most often in a similar industry, so they will already have built up a list of contacts in their proverbial *little-black-book*. This is a great place to start your marketing, provided of course you aren't doing anything dodgy to infringe your employment contract, confidentiality, and patents or anything else. As a general rule we tend to advise clients that if you'd consider sending a personal Christmas Card to someone on your database (as distinct from a card paid for by the business) then it's probably not unreasonable to consider them a part of your own personal database and hence fair game to contact them about your new project. But care is still recommended.

In product terms, most new businesses will provide a *Me-Too* copy product or service, so they then just get a chance to stand out via the detail in their message and communications or by doing things just a bit better. Plus if you talk to the people you already know, it's an opportunity for a personally tailored, and therefore relevant, communication. And that's all fine as it adds up to the potential of relatively easy and free marketing.

This simple approach is also ideal if you haven't yet even fully launched or formulated your business proposition as it lends itself to being a good route to test a new business concept before quitting the day job!

Obviously I didn't do that, but any sensible person would and should!

NB. This actually sparks an interesting thought. It's much easier to start a new business when you are already running one, as the bulk of your risk and costs can be subsidized by the existing business, assuming it's modestly profitable.

Back to the plot.

Some products are of course easier to bring to market than others, and by that we mean quicker and cheaper. Some ideas will have more market potential, that is number of prospective customers, some will have a greater frequency of purchase and repurchase or simply a higher ticket value or referral rate. If you weigh up all these considerations you can start to calculate a potential *Lifetime Value* of the impact and amount of revenue a single client can bring to your business – this should be used to balance against the effort, risk and cost you need to Invest.

Maybe that job in the circus is starting to look a whole lot more appealing instead?

Or stick with your current boss and ask for a pay increase!

But assuming you're made of braver stuff let's get back to the concept of FREE marketing. Hopefully you'll see that not all business ideas are equal and not all of them will need the same marketing push to create sales or sign-ups. Some might be hugely expensive, for example to replicate the marketing strategies of competitors, others can be much more niche and therefore from a financial investment, a lot less risky personally. There is no sense in betting the family house as security for loans or overdraft facilities to fund marketing and sales if you don't need to or if you're not an expert, which increases the risk further, again I didn't do this either – I launched businesses in areas I know nothing about. But it could so easily have gone wrong and lost us Haining Towers.

So do you need marketing? Let's look at an example where you might not.

If you've decided on a business or service that is almost unique and can combine this with an existing good reputation and contacts, it may be as simple as getting your name out through updating (or creating) your LinkedIn profile or contacting a trade journalist for a bit of free PR. Do this and the world might just beat a path to your door. This alone could be enough to get you started, and you can save up for marketing once you start to grow. It's easy to top up this kind of DIY approach with occasional news or thought-provoking short articles that will always sit closer to your knowledge than any outsourced supplier. So you certainly don't need an expensive Marketing agency to do this for you.

That guy who extinguishes oil-rig fires springs to mind as a perfect contender, Red Adair? His skill is almost unique (who else would drive a bulldozer loaded with TNT into a fire!?) and it's presumably a rare but expensive niche service. He can probably also name his price. Why would he need to bother with an expensive multi-channel marketing campaign, online or otherwise? He wouldn't and hopefully doesn't.

Ditto Evil Knievel, but that's probably giving away my age. Hopefully your planned service is a lot safer than either of these choices.

Most of us of course don't have a niche that's so unique and it's harder than ever to get noticed above all the general marketing and communication noise that increasingly intrudes on our lives – we all like to think our businesses are as unique as we are but the truth is there are usually hundreds of people doing pretty much the same thing. So clever marketing is the name of the game and you can target an effective message online and measure it better than almost any other channel.

As a rule of thumb we've generally found that for every 5,000 people in an area there will generally be at least one business or person trading in your area of expertise, unless it's very niche. This helps focus the mind a bit when deciding on advertising and stops us all believing our own hype.

Summary *– Forget being too sexy or clever, look for opportunities that are easiest to communicate, consider doing it yourself at first. If your business is too hard to explain it's probably too hard to market easily. Test it out on your mum!*

Chapter 2
How to leverage government interference

I thought you said the government might help out or pay?

Well remembered, I did. First off, you may not be aware if you are starting out in business that the government, in the UK at least, is very keen to encourage entrepreneurship as it boosts employment and government coffers through taxes. So provided you can make a good and valid argument they will often reward you with grants and or an advance rebate of development costs or your future VAT. You can use their money to get you started for at least a proportion of your costs. It's certainly worth exploring and I have used this generosity to help fund initial marketing and create jobs several times. Similar schemes exist in many countries, each with a particular flavour of the kind of behaviour they want to encourage in businesses.

On a more negative note, governments all around the world have a nasty habit of meddling and love nothing better than intervening in markets. They often do this to encourage a new sector, so bio-sciences and artificial intelligence (AI) might be good current examples at the time of writing; in the past it could have been silicon chips, flat screen monitors or green initiatives. Whatever, a consequence of any intervention, be it via grants or tariffs and restrictions, is that this unwittingly alters the free market. This will create, almost without exception, peaks and troughs in buyer behaviour which will impact demand (at the government's expense) and from which your business could unexpectedly benefit, provided of course you can tweak your offering to align with what they are trying to achieve.

Just a slight tweak may mean that your product or service is suddenly in an area where the awareness marketing costs are being paid by the government, and your focus is then just on sales conversion. This could obviously increase your competition but reduce your risk – a lot. Think of it like fishing in a pond that unbeknown to you has just been restocked with fish – it won't get any easier and even with other fishermen (or should that be fisherpersons?) present, everyone will take home a good catch.

Recent examples could be PPI, Wind and Solar Energy, Eco light bulbs or Tuition fees. And if we look a little wider into the (alleged) EU world of bent bananas, recent restrictions on the sale of powerful vacuum cleaners and normal filament light bulbs. If you were launching, say, a table lamp business, by suddenly encompassing evolving things like LED, your product will be hitting the public awareness at the right time and the government may even create financial incentives to stimulate that market for you.

And because of the government itself spending to increase awareness (it's a little-known fact but if you add all their various departments' spending together they are usually by far the UK's largest advertisers) you can often cut corners and tackle these emerging opportunities at less cost than usual. So you might need nothing more complex than a leaflet or business card, backed up by a simple single landing page website to prove you're a legit trader. That's a lot less expensive than building, say, an e-commerce website with full checkout, user admin areas, social presence and the other essentials.

GDPR – the General Data Protection Regulation – is another recent government initiative that merits particular comment. It could create opportunities if you can sell products or services that are related to it, but more likely it will pose a barrier to business unless you understand it and incorporate it into your plans.

GDPR is recently implemented data regulations in Europe. In simple terms these say it is simply no longer good enough to have a list of your future marketing prospects in an excel file or on index cards in an old shoe-box at the bottom of your desk. You now need to maintain readily accessible, accurate, and timely information on any people or small businesses (sole traders can generally also be regarded as individuals) that you plan to market to. And you need to ensure they are pleased to receive said relevant communications, and can easily opt out. It's important then to ensure the regulations don't hamper your business before it gets fully established.

Summary — *Look for opportunities around the edges of well publicised market trends or changes, and don't ignore the regulatory environment, keep your data updated and relevant.*

Chapter 3
Buy Cheap Marketing, Buy Marketing Twice?

It is very common for business owners, who are generally pretty good at grasping numbers, to spend a lot of time seeking out the cheapest marketing channel, forever interrogating prices and looking for the smallest variance in their spreadsheets in a search for the Holy Grail – the lowest cost marketing channel. Surely such diligence must lead to the lowest customer recruitment cost or Cost Per Acquisition (CPA)?

This is actually one of the greatest anomalies we've noticed in Marketing and we've yet to see it commented on anywhere else. In general terms….

……IT DOESN'T MATTER WHICH MARKETING YOU DO, IT ALL ENDS UP THE SAME!

We realise you may have to sit down after reading that! Obviously the costs and response rates will vary depending on what you sell and who you sell it too, and mistakes can make campaigns a complete flop. Yes – that's true.

But what we mean is that all things being equal, and completed to a reasonable standard, then as any business is always trying to sell a consistent product or service to a consistent audience, it's pretty much just the marketing CHANNEL that is being varied, and that's where comparisons of strategy start to get interesting.

> Let's say you fancied a bit of Direct Mail, the cost in the post after paper, printing, data and other costs might be £0.75 per unit. This might yield in your market a response of say 1%, so that's a cost per conversion or CPA of a hot lead of £75.00 (£0.75 x 100 / 1)

Now your partner in the next office likes a bit of the old and the new so fancies dabbling with email, Search Engine Optimisation and Trade Shows. A managed email service might be say £0.18 per unit and effective at 0.3% which equates to a cost per figure of £60.00. The SEO might typically come in at a monthly budget of £950 across many keywords and yield £65.00 per resulting lead. And a small Trade Show could cost say £4,000 for a modest stand and hotel accommodation but could be yielding say 50 enquiries, this equals £80.00 each.

There is plainly some variation here between the channels ranging from say £60.00 to £80.00 but we consider these are all in a broadly similar ball-park, as there is no channel that is significantly better than any others by a huge % margin such as 300% better, and yet this is what most business owners expect.

In our view cheap acquisition wants to be at least 50% less costly and as you can see nothing is coming in close to that here.

What this means is that provided you send the right message to the right person in the right way, **the costs may not be dissimilar whichever channel you chose**, provided of course it is not a wholly inappropriate channel or the marketing gets messed up somehow!

We have tested this strategy by intentionally going cheap or branching out way beyond the norm and the costs have either gone awry or the response rate has reflected the lower cost and the CPA is mostly unchanged, but we've also wasted time if not money. As an example, low cost unsold "distress" space at a trade show that attracts a broadly correct audience but isn't where you'd expect to go to buy your service that day (let's say you sell **HR** to engineers and it's an engineers' **marketing** show so might look attractive). You won't feel out of place but you'll notice your competitors by their absence!

Guess what will typically happen? You might have saved 80% on the usual costs, but as it wasn't 100% relevant (they will be in a different buying mind-set), your conversion rate will only be 20% of what you might have achieved at the *correct* HR based show, even though it would have had more competition. So you have sort of saved money but you've achieved less and still spent as much time which means that it is not worth it.

This is why in cities you tend to find all the car dealers in one area, the estate agents in another – when people are in the mood for a car, they will be less likely to buy a house but may indeed be willing to change brand of car.

Our theory is that marketing is arguably a very good test of the principle of supply and demand and that as soon as one channel evidences better rates and lower costs, money and effort follows it quickly and removes any significant opportunity for arbitrage or benefiting versus competitors. On rare occasions when clients do find channels that work uniquely for them at much lower than average cost per conversion, they quickly get copied so the goal then is to *Go Large* and fill your boots while you can, as it rarely lasts.

NB. Two areas of caution to note here – this theory applies to channels that are deemed to be successfully working in promoting the target business products and services. Some channels will of course prove to be a complete flop and totally inappropriate and need to be ruled out as quickly as possible, but amongst those channels that work well, the final cost metrics in our experience will be broadly consistent, **so there is no point buying cheap as buying twice is just more effort for the same reward.** Secondly, uses of the terms CPC and Cost Per Click (that is traffic to your website) and CPA and Cost Per Acquisition need to be treated with caution as these are typically not the same as a finished sale and cash in the Bank. Different businesses tend to be a little liberal in their interpretation, so always focus on the end cost and income earned. Remember also that on average roughly only one in 50 people that visits a website will typically transact in some way.

Summary — *Buying Cheap is generally a waste of time if you use appropriate due diligence. It may save you a small amount of money but could double your time losses.*

Chapter 4
Is *New* Marketing Better Than *Old*?

As an Online Marketer of over 20 years standing (actually mostly sitting) you'd probably assume I'd say it's better all round, but in practice, it depends – don't rule out *old* channels just yet.

Online Marketing does have certain in-built advantages over traditional marketing such as speed and tracking (a campaign can be set up and running in minutes and you can immediately measure where prospects went on your website) but you can just as easily pick up a telephone and dial someone, In my view it's less clear cut.

Response rates will of course also vary by season, holiday periods, weather and year by year but tend to gravitate back to the norm if you keep trying year after year – so don't rule out any marketing channel on one poor result.

So rather than say one channel is better than another, let's look at some other notable differences:

> Back to your partner in the next office. She hates direct mail of course but likes loose inserts stuffed in magazines or other people's mailshots as they are less intrusive and wasteful. She knows they typically only cost about £0.10 each to get manufactured and distributed so her assumption is with a similar response rate to mailers (as it's printed communication) you'll achieve a CPA of only £10.00?
>
> No, here is where it gets odd.
>
> This is a less sophisticated approach to the prospect customer, that is it's not addressed, It gets less attention and is actually more likely to

achieve a conversion rate of only say 0.12%, this equates to a cost per figure of say £83.00 (£0.10 x 100 / 0.12) – as so broadly the same ball-park as £75.00 direct mail.

Another colleague likes the intrusive but more personal nature of outbound telemarketing, even though these days it's nigh on impossible to get past the switchboard and talk to a decision maker. His costs per DMC (Decision Maker Contact) are £5.00 per call of which around 7% go on to become leads - so his cost per conversion is £71.00 (£5.00 x 100 / 7)

If we added things like newspaper or magazine advertising, TV adverts, social media adverts etc. into the mix the story remains essentially the same. In some instances the cost of entry or production is huge (such as TV production), but the audience huge, in others the figures are reversed. In almost every case we have seen, the resulting Cost Per Conversion figures remain broadly similar.

We conclude then that no one form of marketing is always better than the other. It depends what you are selling and to whom, plus of course you need an understanding regarding how your prospects like to behave and interact and how complex the buying process, so will it take years during which time they may even access your business multiple times to make up their minds?

I encourage clients to focus more on their own numbers and trying to work out how much a client is really worth to them, both short term and long term, and then developing a marketing strategy that is deployed across relevant multiple channels consistently. This is better than short bursts of activity or channel hopping. Remember also that to close a sale (or whatever is deemed success for your type of business) typically requires a prospective client to interact multiple times (which can be across different channels or media) and this is often over an extended period which can be as much as 24 months.

They might for example receive an initial email, read a newsletter, and talk on the phone and visit an outlet or trade show before transacting with you. Many will of course check out a website to verify that your organisation is genuine and trustworthy, It needs to look credible. Again this points to a multi-channel approach being generally far more successful than putting all your eggs into one basket, be it online or traditional media. And switching horses' mid-race rarely works, it just adds to costs and hassle for everyone.

Please do though note that once a winning channel has been found it is also very common to see the metrics vary due to many external factors that are almost impossible to predict from afar or in advance. This doesn't mean that a channel has necessarily become inefficient or overfished by competitors, it could simply be due to fluctuations caused by external factors that influence buyer behaviour such as the aforementioned changes in weather, school holidays, road-works, the budget, end of tax year etc. In general terms, once a successful channel has been identified it should remain a mainstay of future activity, not binned due to sudden falls in performance which will often be a one off. Instead effort should be committed to continually testing new approaches alongside the winning formula so you always have a Plan B strategy waiting in the wings, and when this starts to fail you have Plan C tested and ready. This constant approach to testing will keep ensuring you have a winning formula that is on trend ahead of competitors.

Summary – *Don't obsess about either finding a rare Holy Grail low cost channel or new or old being best. Be patient, be prepared to test, and be willing to revisit past winners.*

Chapter 5
Local versus National or Global?

 As a business owner or manager it's entirely natural to want the best for your business so by definition that often means you want the largest number of sign-ups, sales or conversions. So that must surely mean when it comes to marketing its obvious you want the biggest catchment area possible so you will want to target an international or at the very least national audience?

This is by no means a dead cert.

Businesses like Google obviously can target a global audience as people everywhere search for everything – but even with a technology-based business like theirs that doesn't interact personally at all with its end customer, that is the searcher, it's not so simple in practice – they may not want international clients.

This could be because in some countries restrictions are imposed on their access, for example China or Korea. In others, internet speeds or server availability and costs won't make it practical to deliver the search service everywhere. And then of course we must remember that whilst the search engines customers are us, that is anyone that searches, in reality the real clients for them are those that pay them, and this will mostly be a local audience in each market. The point we are trying to make is that if even the biggest Internet business of them all doesn't want all the traffic it could get, why would you?

Switch the argument to Amazon and whilst the technical issues are similar, they also have to consider restrictions on e-commerce that countries such as France have imposed, the availability of warehouse space, product suppliers or skilled staff. So even Amazon with its global reach actually wants clients relevant to the catchment of each warehouse in each unique market.

Smaller businesses may have easier issues to grasp but the issues remain the same. I couldn't count on both hands and feet (two of each) the number of times I have been tasked by a business such as a plumber, accountants, financial advisers or Insurers to get them to the top of the Internet on the most significant terms for their respective sector. The Plumber wants to be number one in Google for plumbing, the accountant for terms like payroll or VAT returns, the financial advisor wants to be top for words like pensions, and the insurer probably for house insurance.

In reality many of these businesses require face to face delivery of their product or service and few will have an army of personnel covering the length and breadth of the country. In practice they want a high volume of potential prospects within a suitable drive-time of their business, so tackling international, national or even regional markets may be too much to cope with and a huge waste of resources.

Even if such a result could be delivered cost effectively they will waste time fielding enquiries that the business is ill suited to deliver on, that will annoy people, creating bad will for the brand (which may spread as people love to gossip, especially on social channels) and, of course, it wastes marketing effort and budget.

My advice to clients is always to think very carefully about where you want to deliver your service and target that carefully and fully. As an example a local financial advisor might market themselves around the concept of *London Pensions* or *Wealth Management Brixton*.

If the service can be delivered nationally, say by phone or online application, you'll still want to avoid wasting time and effort fending off the wrong type of prospects. It's very common for lots of prospects to turn out to be people researching a market (students and competitors for example) so you don't want to waste time by targeting such a broad audience.

Taking Insurance as an example, House Insurance could be something being researched and hence prone to wastage, whereas once you drill down to things like *Over 50s' House insurance* or *Studio Flat Insurance* you can imagine being closer to a sale as the topic is focused.

Summary – *Forget vanity high-level global audiences and get as close to your niche as you can. You can tackle the bigger audience later once you've maximised your niche market share and are squirrelling away profits.*

Chapter 6
Understanding Customer Value

Are all prospective customers equal in value?

We have already touched on this earlier in that it is important to understand what a customer is really worth to your business so you can try and balance this equation with an appropriate level of marketing investment and risk.

Let's dig a little deeper.

Firstly we need to consider the costs of marketing and how many touch points a customer will require before committing to a transaction, sale, sign-up or whatever we judge as success.

We then need to understand the amount said customer spends per transaction and the frequency of repurchase of that product or service or revisiting to buy something else.

Opportunities for cross sales or consumables are very important considerations – printer companies sell very inexpensive yet technically complex ink-jet and laser printers as they know once sold we will need to buy overpriced ink cartridges at regular intervals – that's why they make it nigh on impossible to find non-OEM cartridges that work.

Margin earned on products is then a consideration as the largest transaction won't always yield the best profit. Take for example computer manufacturers – they will sell us a highly complex and expensive-to-manufacture laptop for say £300, and they might make £20 profit on this. If you want a second charger cable, that will cost say £30 and might yield £25 profit – but how often have the PC manufacturer or even the retailer tried to upsell you a second cable? Never. It's a missed opportunity to double profits per sale.

And the final part of this important calculation is lifetime value and loyalty. Will the prospect stay with you and buy again? If so, what is the sum total of all these small bits of profit added up? Once you know this you are starting to get close to working out which customers to target.

But we are not entirely finished. I think it's a great idea to also consider a customer's propensity to recommend or refer your business to others, and you can then add the sum total of all their family lifetime values to the customers own value and it brings to life how certain influencers can have a huge impact on your business if you target them correctly or adverse impact if you let them go. Getting noticed by the right kind of bloggers is of course the modern iteration of this – a small number of people who can influence many millions in a positive or negative way.

Is that it?

Well it might be were it not for two extra factors. We are focussing here on positive contributions to your business, be that sales and profit or referrals. It's also important to consider the cost to service a customer as some customers make huge labour demands on staff, customer services, repair teams etc. whereas others never trouble you at all. In many businesses this leads the accountancy teams to study the customer base and shed the 20% most costly to service. This is a great idea provided two further factors have been considered, 1) even loss-making customers may be making a contribution towards the overall running costs of the business, and 2) they could be an influencer of lots of high value customers or buy multiple products from you. Only when the full equation is understood can you make a clear assessment as to whether to walk away from one type of customer.

The final aspect to consider is probably more to do with your plans for your business and how you might exit, than it is purely down to maths. So for example, your business may be more attractive to a potential buyer (if you want to sell it eventually) if you have some big brand names on board, irrespective of their numeric value. Equally when you sell a business you will expect to receive a multiple of turnover or profit in the deal. Depending on how this is structured it may be worth taking on board loss making business or offering radical money back guarantees to boost your numbers!

Summary – *Customers are rarely equal in value and it is vital to work out who you want to target and what behaviours you want to encourage. It's never a bad idea or too soon to also plan for your exit calculation either.*

Chapter 7
Say *No* to Shortcuts

It's really unwise to set out on any marketing project with the idea of finding a shortcut that will save you time and money. In our experience these very rarely exist and can usually be counted upon to deliver failure. In fact we'd go further and say if it's vital to save money and agency suppliers are too expensive, it's better to roll up your sleeves and do the work yourself than go cheap or take shortcuts!

It's of vital importance to work out, as much as you possibly can, that is a degree of near certainty, which will be your:

- USP (Unique Selling Point or Proposition), that is what makes you stand out from all or most of your obvious competition or what is the unique benefit your customers will receive if they work with you?
- A clearly defined message that explains this benefit, not just the features of your business or product. And if you can appeal to buyers' emotions AND logic, not one or the other, so much the better.
- What does your ideal target customer look like? Have an idea about their profile and demographics so that's things like gender, age, occupation, wealth. Better still if you can visualise an imaginary name, status and visual image to help you conjure them up in your mind's eye, making it easier to decide if a planned feature of your campaign feels intuitively right or not.
- Tone of voice is important and will vary depending on whether your prospects are young, old, in work, employed privately or by charity or government. And do you want your brand to have a personality so that

things like a sense of humour or seriousness feel right or inappropriate?

- We have already discussed how the target area is important, so don't cast your net too wide – decide if you want a local niche audience or something wider geographically. If niche, you can talk about the area in your marketing to demonstrate local area knowledge and greater empathy with your buyers.
- Selecting the right product is of course vital and you need to ensure quality lives up to buyer expectations and this ties into whether you have a premium priced or cheap product – each has different expectations but at any end of this spectrum customers expect appropriate value for money and won't thank you if they get mis-sold to or ripped off with a poor product or bad customer experience.

Only when you have a well understood plan in each of these areas, which is something you could articulate to a third party fairly easily, are you ready to jump into marketing.

Summary – *Time spent thinking about the proposition will reap huge dividends later. No short cuts and don't be tempted just to leap into a cheap advertising opportunity that is presented to you at 80% below rate-card prices if you can't work out whether it ticks enough of these points as possible.*

Chapter 8
Planning for Success

In the next section, *Planning for Success*, I will draw together all that we've covered here and take you through the practical steps that are really needed so you can enjoy the success we have brought to our clients.

You've seen already that understanding your market is one key to success and that's my first focus. With all the tools and insights potentially at our disposal now, planning becomes more and important, hence the double meaning in the next Volume's title. You have to have a really strong plan to be successful and you also need to keep in mind all the time why you are planning. Focus on what we've found to be successful – and remember that any time spent planning is rarely wasted, though sometimes it can be frustrating. As we know.

Section 2

Planning for Success

Chapter 9
Understand Your Numbers & Keywords

You will be aware of the old adage, *Fail to plan, plan to fail*. It's certainly true in marketing generally and particularly In online marketing which is a more arithmetic based discipline. In the previous section we have outlined a number of marketing hygiene factors that need to be addressed in developing your plan from a USP and targeting perspective. For Online you also need to ensure you get a specific handle on all of the following.

In the *real* world it's often hard or even impossible to get a handle on the numbers as the data simply isn't available or it's so broad as to be unusable, for example in government or trade body statistics. These sources are still worth checking out as if you can find data close to a sector of interest, it's often free – Year Books are good for spotting changing trends.

In the UK, useful retail data is available such as here https://www.ons.gov.uk/businessindustryandtrade/retailindustry#publications

Beyond government sources, luckily online a lot more data is freely available and whilst it's often not perfect (as the suppliers have an agenda of their own that may not tally with yours) they do at least make some data available – and this again enables you to compare A with B and look at trends to help your decision process. But whichever source you chose it's important to understand that the final real numbers may differ by some magnitude from the data you see, so don't bet the house on it being perfect intelligence. At the end of this book you will find us reference a magic number of 18% as we often find data overstated by 80%+ and 18% is a magic multiplier to correct the numbers!

Imagine the frustration at launching an online business, working out your product and USPs, deciding a target market and then finding you've pushed it at an audience that doesn't exist or you've selected slightly the wrong words and phrases that your prospects just don't use online. You may have used trade jargon, whereas most of them prefer to use layman terms.

This happened in our agency – a client came to us with a great product and a good idea about prospective customers and they had a super website, but back to our fishing example, it was targeted and aimed not at the recently overstocked pond with few fishermen, but the almost empty pond next door that had been overfished for years. It just needed slightly repositioning to attack the right pond!

Tools that can help refine the online potential include:

The Google keyword planner – primarily used to help define PAID advertising campaigns in Google's Pay Per Click (PPC) advertising programme (where you pay for each click to your web page irrespective of whether the prospect subsequently engages with you). This is however also a generally useful tool in helping decide the whole structure of your online business empire and more specifically the words and phrases that should feature in your site. Used sparingly this will help your business get free organic (Search Engine Optimisation) natural traffic without paying for it.

https://adwords.google.com/intl/en_uk/home/tools/key word-planner/

WEALTH WARNING – Google will encourage you to create a paid advertising account that could eat up a lot of your business's marketing budget very quickly – so only take this step when you fully realise what you are getting into and how the budget gets spent. We'd suggest start dabbling with just £100 or $100. Google is also continually hiding more and more data so you need to experiment with this tool a lot to drive out hidden words and phrases, the latest being plurals. Again remember our previous comments about 18% if the numbers feel wrong.

www.Wordstream.com A paid-for tool that helps you further refine keyword lists in a similar way to Google Adwords but is also designed to help reduce your Adwords wastage, as Google won't always tell you reliably!

www.semrush.com Another paid tool with a broad range of analysis tools to give you an insight into who is looking for what online. Many Search Engine Marketing and Search Engine Optimisation agencies use this to provide clients with reports – we think our own www.Interwebbing.com gives more reliable but less glitzy results!

Summary *– It's surprising but in our experience, almost every trade researched has a similar number of practitioners, but they don't all target the same prospects. Get your data targeting right and your audience can often be 1,000% higher than most of the competition.*

Chapter 10
Identify Positive and Negative Online Trends

It is of course not enough to just have an understanding of how much business exists in a given trade sector or even which keywords people are using to find it, it is crucial to also understand whether a sector is in decline or a growth phase. Declining markets may still yield opportunities, for example competitors exit leaving a clearer playing field, but you wouldn't necessarily want to take a long time and spend a fortune gearing up in a declining market versus say a new or growing one.

Luckily, Google can help a bit with their own trend tool, albeit this only works on big data sources, not tightly defined niches.

https://trends.google.co.uk/trends/

This is a free tool that provides an insight into the seasonal changes for a specific phrase based on Google's own data. If you are planning on targeting niche markets then start at a high level (with generic catch-all phrases) to get an idea of the merits of one area over another. As an example, it could help you decide on the merits (in terms of trends) of *insurance* vs *pension*s or *car insurance* vs *house insurance* but is unlikely to be very useful when you drill down to a niche such as *pet insurance Shrewsbury* as it will probably have insufficient data to reveal any trend for this.

Amazon data can also reveal useful insights particularly if you have a retail sector in mind.

Irrespective of whether you plan to sell through Amazon entirely (they stock and sell for you), in part (they sell, you fulfil) or not at all – for example sell direct yourself or via eBay. Two useful paid tools that leverage Amazon data and past trend analysis are:

https://www.junglescout.com/
http://asinspector.com/

Summary — *Don't be frightened by declining trends, but you need to be fully aware of the direction of the sector you are entering before it's too late. It's not unusual to see growing markets in the real world but declining trends online, because the channels are not always in alignment as often sectors that started well online are now becoming a bit boring and people are drifting back to other channels like mail order.*

Chapter 11
Research Your Competitors

A number of the aforementioned tools can also be used to give an insight into how your competitors **may** be performing, we've highlighted that as the data will never be 100% accurate (just as if you ask them how things are going they are very unlikely to give you a totally accurate or complete verbal answer!)

Alexa is also worth checking out – yes, the same Amazon owner as the Alexa we love to talk to, but *No*, it's not actually the same gadget! This originated as a free toolbar and download many years ago and which was used by tech savvy developers and technicians to combine web usage behaviour and provide anonymised aggregated data in return. It still pretty much does that, albeit in different ways now (as Amazon has bucket loads of data at its disposal both through its own businesses and maybe if you believe in Big-Brother via all its cloud hosting for big brands).

Either way, we think it's always worth checking out what Alexa (the toolbar, not the kitchen gadget) can reveal about a website, if its big and or important enough, but we still recommend assuming the data in Alexa may be slightly skewed towards a technical audience, so not exactly the same as Joe Public.

https://www.alexa.com/siteinfo/johnlewis.co.uk   This enables you to check out competitors and get a rough feel for how far up the Internet greasy pole they are relative to each other. Only large websites have enough data to show graphs for example, hence the example of John Lewis.

The **Wayback Machine** at archive.org is a useful way of getting a look at a snapshot of competitors' sites at a point in the past, even if said business is closed now. The URL should still lead you to this valuable data archive.

https://archive.org/ So let's say you plan to start selling washing machines online, you could check out how Comet was doing it years ago in October 2012 just before they closed down forever that year.

https://web.archive.org/web/20121016021017/http://www.comet.co.uk:80/s/Kitchen-Home/Laundry-Dishwashers/1680

Summary – *It's surprising how often a seemingly new strategy has in fact been tried before, without success. Now may of course be the right-time, right-place – but better not to jump without looking!*

Chapter 12
Beware Search Engine Data

Don't expect Google or Amazon to share all their secrets.

Whilst any of the Online mega-businesses (Google, Amazon, Bing, Facebook, LinkedIn, Pinterest, Twitter) can provide a useful source of intel to aid your business strategy and marketing planning, they all have an agenda of their own (generally to get you to part with money somehow) so don't expect them to be fully transparent with any data shared, or if they give your business a personal helping-hand, don't expect their agents to be anything other than *on commission*.

It won't always be true of course, but it will help safeguard your marketing budgets for a bit longer if you expect this bias.

Common issues encountered include:

Not all the data will be made available to you.

This is *overt* as in the case of Google intentionally hiding more and more browser source data under the tab of *Not Provided*. (You can of course learn more if you are a big budget spender under their Adwords program.) And we have already mentioned recent moves to hide plural data (or show plural but omit singular search terms).

This can be *covert*. As if by magic, data you suspect must exist will be hidden when you interrogate the systems — typically this will be the cheapest leads or lowest estimated conversion cost traffic, hence pushing advertisers to more expensive areas with a lower return on investment (ROI).

The secret is to keep varying your input criteria around the topic of interest (so keep researching a subtly and slightly different audience) and keep retrying at different times of day. Gradually you should then be able to compile a much fuller picture. We generally conclude we haven't finished our research in a market unless we have identified over 2,000 potential search terms.

They will also tend to push you towards a broader market.

Wherever possible these large marketing businesses (as that's what they really are) will impress you with big numbers, making online advertising look like a dead cert? *How can we lose if we get another 9,305 enquiries to our website each month? that's 300 a day!*

This tends to encourage activity targeting a broader market than necessary and also encourages a large total marketing spend – this is the same strategy as estate agents or realtors over-valuing your property to make you choose them.

Real value is achieved not by targeting the masses but by targeting the largest available niche you can find. Such an audience will be more relevant to your message and hence should also be more likely to engage with your business, purchase, join, for example. This higher purchase rate may lead to a higher *cost per* figure than bigger broad data per unit, but that is not always the case. In many cases niche data has both a lower acquisition cost per click and a higher sales conversion rate – so as you can imagine this creates a much lower Cost Per Acquisition (CPA) and is good news for you, bad news for the online giant selling you data.

Let's bring this to life a little more using the terms mentioned in our section on trend analysis.

A high-level term like *insurance* might have a cost per click of £1 and yield clients (as it's too general) at a rate of 0.1% = a CPA of £1,000. But you might pay for loads of clicks.

The more targeted *car insurance* might be £1.90 but yield at 2% equals a CPA of £95. Again volumes will be large.

The term that won't work in the trends tool, *pet insurance Shrewsbury* might have a click price of just £0.10p, but be highly relevant if you were in Shrewsbury so could convert at 20%, giving a cost per acquisition of just £0.50

If you buy clicks, they may overcharge you.

This is one reason why we are advocates of natural organic Search Engine Optimisation (SEO) where all clicks and traffic should be free (aside from your fixed monthly agency fee of course) so there is no chance of being overcharged for an alleged visit to your site. In fact over time the CPA should drop as volume grows for an unchanged monthly fee, irrespective of volume.

With paid advertising it's a whole different ball-park and it is in the interests of the data seller to charge you for as much data and visitors as they possibly can, and for as many terms as possible as this builds the traffic volume, irrespective of whether they transact with your business. Whilst they can and should (in theory) eliminate things like repeated clicks from the same IP address (this could be your competitor intentionally clicking your *advert* to use up your budget), they're not that reliable at doing so and we know of at least one client who has successfully challenged, sued and won a case for excessive charges from a major search engine, so be on your guard.

Also with paid advertising whilst you typically sign up to purchase an agreed number of visitors or clicks (rather than for a period of time) the actual number delivered is subject to estimates. It's not unheard of for search engines to deliver more than had been purchased – and unlike an online supermarket who would refund you for over delivery, they will still charge you beyond your expected budget. Lovely.

Summary — *If you go into online marketing thinking all the data is a bit suspect and everyone is after your budgets, you won't go far wrong!*

Chapter 13
Lifetime Value – Repeat Sales or One Trick Ponies?

Anyone who has studied *old marketing* will most probably often drift back to thinking of the world in terms of Customer Loyalty and Lifetime Value, so basically once you get a prospect converted to your business, if you treat them well, offer quality and value, they will then reward you with a lifetime of business (which has a profit value, hence Lifetime Value). They may also recommend your services to all and sundry, creating an even higher Total Wealth Value.

In my early career in banking for HSBC this concept was embodied in the process of checking customers' account balances and marrying that up into how they were treated, beyond just being treated with respect, obviously.

Not only could you instantly look up how much money they had available, you could see what was going through the pipeline (as a debit or credit) to give an estimate of the future value in a few days' time. You could also check out the total of all their *other* accounts combined within the Bank and its subsidiaries (NB. Banks generally have a largely unknown All-Monies clause in their contracts which gives them a right to offset your other credits to pay your debts, should the need arise. Don't always put all your eggs in one basket – it's a good idea to consider splitting your business and personal banking with different Banks).

But the Bank went a stage further. Through a concept called Connected Accounts, they also flagged your family accounts, friends, business contacts, in fact any relationship where you had possible hidden influence – and we could see the whole sum of these accounts added together so we'd know the risk if we bounced a cheque for a small amount. This taught us that even if a customer only had £100 to their name, through connections, if they were treated badly, we could be putting at risk say £1m worth of business. Now that's a real understanding of lifetime value, especially if combined with referrals over the years and all those combined values too.

Whilst this kind of concept should be easier in today's world of interconnected technology and CRM systems, it's anything but. Data Protection probably compounds the difficulty of treating you better because of your auntie's wealth, Frequent Flyer or Amazon Prime status. But the concept remains valid even if the tracking ability doesn't!

Sadly whilst data protection and other issues have seen little progress in getting to grips with Lifetime Value, another shift in consumer behaviour has impacted all this – we are all a lot more impatient, "I want it and I want it now," is the mantra. Plus we have become nations of disloyal canny shoppers always seeking out the lowest price. It's now the norm to repurchase from an entirely new supplier, either because of a better deal or simply because a bewildering array of choice makes it harder than ever to recall where you last purchased something, unless it was Amazon or eBay of course.

This leads us on to a very important point about Online Marketing. Many business owners, being a little older, tend to have one foot still in the Consumer Loyalty and Lifetime Value camp, so they believe their business, be it old or new, will gain lots of new shiny customers and then can keep marketing to them and milking them for years – effectively mining the lifetime value even if they are not that good at mining it all. This is rarely the case and hence a huge mistake if customers turn out to be disloyal even after receiving a great service.

These businesses can end up spending too much to acquire a new customer with a high CPA (in the hope or expectation of some upside lifetime value later, for it not to materialise) only to find disloyalty, poor memory, or simply a desire for change or a bargain will drive customers away. This is probably what led to the death of businesses like the aforementioned Comet and it's certainly what helps prop up inflated Cost Per Click advertising prices through channels like Google Adwords as most businesses do not realise that through highly effective and aggressive monetarisation, more than all the profit has already been extracted from the margins within said traffic.

The important key here is to regard each lead or client as a one-trick-pony that will in all probability not buy from you again. If you can make money from them under those circumstances, you are on your way to online success. And of course every occasional customer that bucks the trend and does still then return or recommend is pure profit to your bottom line.

Having gone on at length about this it is worth adding some caveats that can work to your advantage.

Modern marketers, especially online, do not seem, in the main to have **any awareness whatsoever** of lifetime value. They only think transactionally and that a customer will buy just once, so they then focus attention on winning the next customer, not selling again to the old one. It's sensible to think this way given the point made previously re disloyalty but does not mean businesses should waive all attempts at getting some repeat business, as the profits on this will be disproportionately high.

Ignoring lifetime value altogether is also a huge and costly mistake given the huge acquisition costs. This creates a fantastic opportunity if you can identify products and services with an inbuilt but unexpected propensity to encourage loyalty and resales at low cost, which may not be so obvious to younger marketers.

Things like ink-jet printers make the point but aren't so easy in practice as they are a manufactured product – but we can understand they are probably sold at a loss, or at best break-even, in the hope we will all buy original cartridges for a lifetime, at huge profit margins, and many of us do.

Things like shavers and refills or devices that require a certain type of oil or cream to function also fit the bill, plus of course ongoing membership to service plans and clubs or magazines.

If you can possibly sell a product that then forces clients back to you, you can break out of this single sales nightmare and if you are confident of your ability to upsell and unlock lifetime value at minimal extra cost and effort, you can take a longer-term view on where your break-even cost point is for a new customer acquisition. You can set yourself deeper pockets and longer timescales than your short sighted misguided *modern* competitors. We have seen this time and time again with *old* marketers who have traditionally been slow out of the starting blocks into online marketing but are now making huge gains as they know how to upsell with ease.

If you are an old-fashioned catalogue marketer, come on in, the online water's choppy but lovely!

Summary – *Think low value short term customer relationships or seek out products and services with easy higher lifetime upsell potential, but don't inadvertently mix the two.*

Chapter 14
Online Budget Setting and Quick Tools

The general approach to deciding on an online marketing budget seems to be to stick a finger in the air, assess the wind speed, and guess, usually to the client's detriment. It may be an acceptable approach for quotes from back-street mechanics and dodgy builders but we believe in a professional sector like marketing, it should be a bit more, well, professional.

OK. I've now admitted I'm old fashioned in writing!

Many years ago we developed a simple (sadly not simple enough to reproduce here) algorithm and macro that uses Google's own data to help work out the respective difficulty of one keyword versus another and turn this into an hourly estimate of time required to work on optimising it each month. And of course time can be turned into budget suggestions. More about this tool in a minute when we have set a bit of context for you.

The other common way to decide on a online marketing budget is of course to trust Google via its own Ad-sales tool in the Adwords program, or you can use Bing. It's generally a bit cheaper but with around 20x less traffic, most marketers ignore this until they have run out of capacity within Google or competitors have pushed the bid prices per click too high at Google.

So how does Google's Pay Per Click (PPC) work and is it a good thing?

With Paid Search you are picking words or phrases relevant to your business, creating mini adverts that sell the sizzle of your business, placing these in Google so they show when said words are searched on, and then if your *advert* is clicked you pay a small fee (circa £0.10-£2.00) to drive them to the page you feel is most relevant on your site. If they leave quickly or buy, that's for you to worry about, not Google, but they won't like it if customers bounce back quickly as it means they were dissatisfied.

Seems good?

Paid search does indeed have several big advantages going for it, firstly, you can adopt a DIY approach and get started yourself without any interference. It's a good plan as even if you waste a few pounds it puts you in a better position later to understand what Marketing Agencies or Consultants are telling you generally, that is not just about PPC, and makes it more likely you'll spot a scam or wolf in marketer's clothing!

You could even get started with £100, and if you type into Google **"Adwords Promo codes"** followed by your country. You will typically get a free trial voucher from them and Bing to get you hooked!

It also has the advantage of speed, as campaigns can be set up and generally approved (if you follow simple rules) very quickly.

And the final plus is that as results are obvious, that is I paid some money, I received X clicks through to my website within a few hours or days, and it led to Y sales or enquiries (if fully tracked) then you can see where your money is going, and quickly test new ideas and strategies.

The downsides? Isn't their always one?

There are three, probably four main ones.

Firstly, once started it becomes a hard habit to break (even if other channels can deliver a lower acquisition cost why take the risk of testing something else? And the search engines rely on this buyer inertia).

Secondly, the minute you stop spending you stop advertising and your competitor (who can easily see what you are doing) steps into your shoes at the top within seconds, while they have money to spend. And as you'd expect, this tends to lead to a bidding war where the profit margin in a click is eroded and the only winner is Google, or Bing. In our experience, in many markets, the competition has already eroded all the profit margin.

The search engines set the bid prices based on a range of factors which include competition and of course their perception of the quality of your business and its website – this is as it serves no one's best interests to push customers to pages they won't like and won't *action* by buying something or joining, irrespective of whether you pay a lot for the click. This supposed *quality score* also maximises the search engines' profits – surprise surprise, who'd have thought that!

The search engines also control the data that their keyword analysis tools display to you, and choose which priced keywords you will see (hence our earlier suggestions to repeatedly re-interrogate these tools to unearth hidden terms by varying subtly what you are searching for) and may hide things like singular or plural terms even though they are obviously being searched on.

In summary, PPC tools are a good way of assessing how much you might spend on paid search and despite the issues they seem to be the main means by which most businesses get a feel for how much they need to spend on online marketing campaigns. It is however worth remembering that paid advertising represents only around half the market, so whilst other channels may deliver a cheaper cost per acquisition, if you want to blanket cover the whole potential market, you probably need to at least **double** how much the paid engines suggest, irrespective of whether you are aiming to do the work via an agency or in-house.

In our experience, it is now pretty typical for businesses to spend around **10-12%** of actual or anticipated turnover on marketing, this is up from circa 3% at the start of the decade. With margins under constant pressure it further confirms the importance of putting the effort into your *marketing planning* at the outset. The split of online versus offline will vary based on product, service, price, audience, and location but assuming 50% and 50% is a good place to start, that is half the budget is on old school real-world things, and half is online.

We talked earlier about our algorithm that enables us to predict ideal SEO budgets. In general they would represent around a quarter of the business's total marketing budget (as circa 45% should normally be SEO) the rest split between a similar amount on PPC, and the balance on website maintenance, email and other online opportunities. Plus of course the initial set up costs of establishing a website in the first place – costs here vary from **say £2k** for a simple but good *brochure* website that promotes you well, through to **£20-£30k** for a fully functioning e-commerce trading website or content management or bespoke database system. The upper end can of course go a lot higher for big organisations, huge audiences or user numbers or be a lot cheaper for a DIY template-driven approach.

If you are still a little stuck when it comes to defining budgets for your new online activities we would commend you to test out each of the following that will give you an annual ball-park to start with (and we have proven these over many years' experience and hundreds of successful campaigns):

Quick Calc One. What is **10%** of the cash balance generally available in your business? This often seems to be a spare buffer that won't put the business at risk if its committed to marketing online.

Quick Calc Two. What is **5%** of the business's end of year Asset Value or Net Worth? Similar to the cash value, our experience has shown one twentieth of the businesses asset value seems equivalent to the spare buffer, so often agrees with calculation One above.

Not As Quick – Calc Three. Compile a keyword target list using Adwords or SEMRush, multiply the Average Monthly Traffic for each term X Competition% x Cost Per Click, and divide the resulting total by either **TWO** (or if you know said term's position in Google, by that number, for example 5 if you were in 5th place on page 1 for that term or 12 if you were in 2nd place on page 2). Then add all the resulting totals together and divide by twelve.

The spread of these answers generally represents a good start point for setting a **monthly** SEO budget, and you shouldn't find too big a variance across the methods. Multiply the answer by 2.2 or so if you are trying to set your first total marketing budget and are an established business, with a bit more for a new start-up.

Sorry: we didn't say it was easy, hence why most people just guess or trust Google!

Summary – *Budget setting needn't be guess work. Have a dabble yourself with Adwords and then use that as a basis for understanding how you might pick a PPC, SEO and overall budget that at least has a semblance of science and should be affordable for most businesses. Or just use your cash and asset value as a guide, but ensure you have a plan.*

Fail to plan, plan to waste money.

Chapter 15
Good Versus Bad Savings

With the huge expense of marketing it is so tempting to cut any corner you can and many businesses do, and that's probably not helping the very low survival rate of businesses in their first five difficult years.

If you have almost unlimited budgets then plainly you need to cut back on nothing. Great. That should get you top notch advisers and guaranteed success! For everyone else on a budget we will comment below on the most common pitfalls we have seen which have restricted businesses' success online:

Cheap URLS (web names)

Cheap universal resource locators (URLs) generally come from low cost hosting suppliers. Aside from the obvious fact that these companies often have poor customer support (so can't or won't help when simple things go wrong, which they often do online) you will generally find prices rise on renewal to a higher unit cost than the average, so eroding any apparent saving unless you plan on selling the URL in a couple of years. In our view it's cheap for no good reason.

The big issue here isn't just the cost or support but also that cheap suppliers often configure URLs in a way that is search engine unfriendly or they simply don't have the means to technically keep up with changes that search engine algorithms require in later years.

With URLs probably costing no more than 0.05% of the running costs of your business, this is a saving you don't need chase and shouldn't. Man-up and pay an extra £10 a year, honestly it's worth it.

Offshore Hosting

When we started working online URLs cost circa £200 each and hosting was tens of thousands of pounds per annum, but as technology gets smarter and cheaper, storage costs have fallen and you can now host sites for minimal cost, or even for free if you get space from your email provider or telco for example. But this does not mean it's a good deal, for two main reasons.

Firstly, low cost hosting typically comes with minimal help, this also extends to the type of programming or software that can be readily be supported as business-as-usual, so for example, you may have website requiring WordPress only to discover your hosting won't support certain WordPress themes or plug-ins, or it won't be updated often enough, making it useless to you.

Even worse is if the hosting package has its own bespoke website builder software – this is almost guaranteed to be search engine unfriendly, so you will waste your time building a website that will only ever get found by people you tell about it directly (so do you even need a website? More on that later) and will never get found by potential customers searching for what you do, not who you are.

The second reason for avoiding low cost offshore hosting is that all things being equal, when the search engines have to present a browsing customer with a search result, they will tend to display first those results coming nearer from home, both by country and region or town. This is for the simple reason that people tend to prefer to shop local and isn't it likely if you were, say, in the UK, you would prefer to transact with or join a website that is in your home country than say one in the USA or France? Local results will also be delivered fractionally quicker, and speed is one of the most critical factors influencing Google and other search engine algorithms.

It is of course possible to optimise a website so this is less likely to happen (for example if you need to target an international audience with particular parts of your website) but in most cases it is fairly safe to assume as standard that you will be better off in the long run if you find a reputable local hosting supplier. And if you plan a large multi-national business at some point you will need to consider bespoke content in each country.

Shared Servers

Related to the issue of cheap offshore or free hosting is the concept of shared hosting – it's a fairly typical scenario but not without its own pitfalls. Shared hosting does what it says on the tin: you are sharing your hosting with other businesses, so it's a bit like lending your laptop to your children or neighbours, except that you might not know who they are!

Shared servers came about because years ago it could easily cost say £20k per annum for a dedicated website server – this cost being made up of a combination of hardware purchase costs, rack-space rental costs, energy and telephony bills to connect the server onto the Internet plus of course maintenance costs to manually set-up and keep an eye on things. This was a cost only the largest businesses could afford so the concept of sharing seemed a good idea – the server space was rented out in partitions, a little like having different folders in your filing cabinet. Each folder was used for its own unique purpose and website (within boundaries of software functionality), and centralised costs were split between users, often on a basis of bandwidth used. In the early days, this caused few problems and with servers having a few hundred websites, all sharing a similar IP address, it was rarely a problem.

But things online rarely stay the same, as competition increased so did the pressure to create ever more attractive, or free, hosting packages so it's now not unknown to have 4,000 websites all sharing one server. As you can imagine, the likelihood of any one of these sites dominating said server due to having faster growth in user numbers or downloads, for example if the content was suddenly topical or in the news, or having technical issues due to loading incorrect software, is magnified. This will impact Google and other engines' general view of that server and its associated IP addresses, so your site has the potential to be slowed down, and hence held back by the engines, because of your many neighbours' good or bad performance. This would be bad enough if you knew your neighbours and had some say in what they are doing, but you don't get that – you won't easily know who you share with, what they do, and if they are being viewed positively or negatively.

We will touch on the concept of bad neighbours in the next section but suffice to say it is always a good idea online to know who your business is being associated with, intentionally or otherwise.

Bespoke servers, that is just used by your business, are now a lot more affordable. Used rack or blade servers can be acquired from around £500 with new ones in the £1000-£4000 price range. Alternatively, they can be supplied and hosted by a company such as 1and1co.uk or *WPBeast.co (one of our trusted partners) for* around £40 per month (as at Feb 2018, prices will generally be expected to drop) so it's worthwhile these days considering having space just for yourself.

Cheap developers

As you can probably tell from all the aforementioned pitfalls of buying cheap it is vital to ensure that your website is run on up to date software and systems so that it can be more easily found by the search engines – this is unless you have intentionally taken a strategic decision that this does not matter and you do not need to be found.

Whilst it is good to hire the services of a developer as cheaply as possible it is far preferable to get a special deal from a good proven developer or web designer than it is to simply purchase from a cheap supplier – in our experience the latter will rarely have the time to keep up with developments online in which case your business will forever be on the back-foot. And it's never a good idea to end up paying your supplier by the hour to learn something they should know already as business-as-usual!

Summary *– Strike good supplier deals wherever you can but try and avoid buying any services needed online purely on price alone. It will cost a lot more to rectify the problems later and you may even end up having to start from scratch all over again.*

Chapter 16
Think BIG?

By now it is understandable if the complexities of online trading are seeming so bad that the obvious solution is simply, borrowing a McDonald's analogy, to go LARGE or buy everything you need from a large supplier, be that an agency or software vendor. This could be true if you have deep pockets and are building a global brand, but in most cases it simply won't represent great value for a number of surprising reasons.

Large agencies have large overheads and are geared to dealing with large clients with substantial annual budgets. They are therefore unlikely to be keen working with smaller businesses demanding answers quickly and will often appoint office juniors or even trainees at lower hourly charge out rates to cut their teeth and learn on the campaign when they are supposed to be leading it! They will have big job titles and seem suitably professional, but scratch the service of the individual, not the agency, and they will often be found wanting in the detail.

In contrast, with a smaller agency of similar size to your own business they will often be able to dedicate senior staff with experience to your campaign and be more familiar with the pressures in a new or smaller business.

From a software perspective, even if you are committing £hundreds of thousands per annum, it is not uncommon for the largest software systems used by very large organisations, to be several years behind the curve and hence not at all search engine friendly.

This is not dissimilar to how you will notice when buying a new car, the fitted satellite navigation will generally be a couple of years behind the sophistication of the versions sold as stand-alone accessories. The reasoning is simple – these organisations are so huge with so many interlocking departments, complexities and goals that it takes them years to research, plan and react to market changes whereas smaller suppliers can be much more responsive and fleet of foot. When these huge systems are deployed, seemingly simple changes can often take months and cost £1000s whereas in smaller suppliers a similar task would be completed in hours for £50.

We are aware that one of the suppliers of market leading e-commerce software (who needs to remain nameless for legal reasons) used by many of the world's leading brands is at least 3 years behind in SEO technology and not a single one of their clients' websites will be capable of easy optimisation to get found – so clients are wasting millions in wasted marketing to make up for the software shortcomings. In fact Google is building systems in the opposite strategic direction to the development plan of said supplier! Now strangely if you talked to the Head Office of either the software supplier themselves or their buyers they would all be confident they are at the leading edge of SEO – this is where big company arrogance prevents them from any belief that they could be anywhere but at the front of the game.

Summary – Unless you have millions to burn you will not achieve best value by picking the biggest suppliers and best-known brands if you want to get found online. It's better to be the biggest fish (client) within a smaller pond (agency) as you will generally be able to command the time of the Directors or stakeholders, not just junior staff.

Chapter 17
Your Website

In the next section, *Your Website*, I'll reveal everything we've learnt about websites over the years and what practical steps you have to take to make your website stand out and contribute to business success.

The world of websites is changing faster and faster – just like everything else online – but people tend to stick to what they know or what they found successful years ago. Fashions in website design change relatively quickly, and it's useful to know how to stay up to date.

More importantly, you may find that you stub your metaphorical toes on things that seem relatively simple – like migrating your website to a new environment. It's that sort of technical and business snag that I go into in practical detail in my next short book.

Section 3
Your Website

Chapter 18
Do You Need an Expensive Website?
Do You Really Need the Expense of a Website at All?

We've talked about the various ways of marketing your business, both traditionally and online, now let's looks specifically at that most common of online activities for businesses, the website itself. And by website, we mean the old-fashioned approach consisting of a series of interconnected pages grouped under a common web name and Unique Resource Locator (URL).

It is a common assumption that these days, that, to be modern, every business obviously needs a website.

Actually, that's no longer entirely true.

Sure, a few years ago any respectable business would be expected to have a few pages about themselves, explaining what they do, credentials, products and of course the all-important contact details page. Such sites, being non-transactional with no need for sophisticated back-office order systems, shopping baskets or even content management and editorial systems are often referred to as online brochure sites. And that's exactly what they are, an online brochure or extension of your business card which people generally reference to check up the status and validity of your business, in other words, that you actually exist and look credible. It's all stuff and nonsense of course as any dodgy person can spend a few pounds on acquiring a professional looking website, hence the phrase you may have heard: "Nobody can tell if you are a dog on the Internet!"

An online brochure site like this can of course be a DIY project using a tool like www.wix.com or website builder at www.1and1.co.ukwebsite-builder and can cost just £1 a month or even be entirely free if you avoid all the additional modules. Or you could pay a little more for a service from say www.squarespace.com (not forgetting our comments about hosting location of course).

Needless to say, but we'll say it to be extra clear, these are fairly limited websites in terms of overall capability (they can still look very professional) as the platform on which they are built is limited. You shouldn't expect them to also have all the up to date functionality to enable them to be fully optimised and updated on an ongoing basis as you would with an expensive bespoke build. You will of course also be sharing space with thousands of other websites, and we have already talked about the risks with that approach, so whilst these kinds of sites have limitations, they are certainly worth considering if your budget doesn't stretch to say the £2,000 a good web developer will charge for a more advanced version, using say WordPress or developed bespoke in PHP and html.

The important thought to remember here is that with a low-cost site you will most likely need to rely on paid advertising or your own real-world networking to drive visitors in any significant volume – so regard the website as a support for your other marketing, **not** the marketing itself!

As the Internet has evolved there are however many new ways of having an online presence that don't rely on having a website which you need to modestly or expensively maintain, both in terms of budget and time. Whatever you do online still requires effort and commitment of course, but these days you can avoid the expense and hassle of website ownership yet have an entirely appropriate modern online persona by adopting instead any of the following:

Create an **eBay** shop

https://sellercentre.ebay.co.uk/business/open-shop

Or sell via **Amazon** – they can even manage fulfilment for you

https://services.amazon.co.uk/services/sell-online/how-it-works-pro.html

NB. These channels can charge up to 35% margin on sales, so be careful!

Via a dedicated **Facebook** business page

 https://www.facebook.com/business/learn/set-up-facebook-page

NB. Facebook also owns **Instagram**, and this site has potential to help promote businesses particularly in the media industries.

Templates enable a stylish **blog** to be created on platforms such as:

www.wordpress.org – this has lots of plug-ins to increase functionality although you may need specialist paid-for advice to add these on and not every plug-in works with every one of them. WordPress is also used by many web developers as the underlying platform (as its quick to build once you learn the ropes) not that all their clients will realise this.

www.blogger.com – although this has both the advantage and disadvantage or being owned by Google (you'd assume this increases visibility but it's not guaranteed as Google often loses interest in its previous acquisitions!)

www.Tumblr.com – the big plus is this is a free platform and has good links into social channels generally; the downside is it has limited capability or room to grow.

www.Linkedin.com started life as a free and easy way for business people to keep in touch with each other as in essence it was an online business card (and if you changed your employer or contact details, everybody you were connected too would be alerted). This morphed into a business enabling users to source and contact persons-of-interest through the concept of six degrees of separation whereby everybody on the planet can be reached through the friends of friends of no more than 5 people. It has since been acquired by Microsoft and is now aligned around paid-for membership. Notwithstanding this recent limitation the service does allow free membership and you can create a free mini business portfolio site at:

www.linkedin.com/company/setup/new

For business in creative industries with unique one-off products to promote, then www.Etsy.com is a good option offering the ability to create an online listing for yourself and your products without monthly fees and just a modest listing fee. They also charge a transaction fee on sales but generally it works out a little bit cheaper than EBay:

www.etsy.com/uk/sell?ref=hp

For some businesses there may be at least 7 alternatives to consider to just a *traditional* website, all of which may save you money and in many cases they will help drive potential customers to you in return for their share of your cake. And of course you don't need to limit yourselves to only picking one of these.

If you do still opt for a bespoke website of your own, these options can be considered alongside your website, moving you into the realms of being a multi-channel business before you've even started. How exciting is that?!

NB. One extra point to remember is that when you are building a site in a platform or hosting scenario, such as Blogger, in general terms you are unlikely to be building up a strong SEO profile for your individual business but will be increasing the profile of the host organisation – so they will gain higher positions in Google searches, and you won't.

Summary – *For many businesses there is no need to rush into the expense of creating a bespoke website, but strings are attached. Also if you opt for this route expect to have to invest in a stand-alone website later once your business grows, so you'll be spending resources twice but at least by then it should be funding its own success and growth.*

Chapter 19
What's In a Name?

We've all been stuck in traffic behind a van with the most ridiculously long web address or email – something impossible to remember (so you need to take a photo to recall it later!) or attached to a web service that is so old it's probably extinct, so things like:

www.JoesPlumbersNorthamptonshire.Freeserve1006.co. uk or www.Joe7649@AOL.com

Needless to say these don't convey the most professional of images so if you have decided you need your own bespoke website with its own URL (as distinct from a template page elsewhere where you generally get told what address you can have), then it's worth giving some detailed thought to the choice of name.

Short names and easy to spell words generally work best, or if you have a bigger budget so can spend money creating awareness, then its fine to go with a made-up word, so as an example **Shpock** or **Trivago**, although TBH we hate both of these as they are almost impossible to remember how to spell, never a great idea. At least businesses like Yahoo had the decency to pick words that did at least exist in the dictionary, albeit not in common parlance.

For most businesses then we recommend picking something simple, preferably easy to recall, and if it's possible to say-what-it-means on the tin, so much the better. So Speedy Northampton Plumbers would fit that description really well.

Needless to say all the best web names will have been used already, either by genuine users or cyber squatters hoping to sell it on for a profit. In general it is best to purchase a

URL for the country in which you are based or where you plan to trade, so in our case that's, **co.uk**. Second best would be to get the much sought after .com American web address as in most countries of the world, **.com** is seen with as much credibility as a home based URL. Unless you are a charity, in academia or in government we strongly recommend **all other types of URL extension are avoided like the plague**, however cheap they are, however tempting it may be to get exactly the name you want, or however compelling the salesperson. The same can be said for avoiding hyphens if at all possible. This is for several reasons.

First and foremost, it's not what most users expect to see – so even if they can remember your business name, they will type in the wrong extension or miss the hyphen, and presumably arrive at your competitors. It's also not really what Google and other search engines like to see and at the time of writing they appear to give significant extra weight in their algorithms to *traditional* URLs. In fact we'll go further and say we suspect that some of the newer lesser known URL extensions aren't even indexed by the major search engines at all.

NB. This does not mean you should avoid buying lesser quality web addresses or extensions – they are worth acquiring to block out your competitors – but they should not be used for your main web address and please don't **ever** be tempted to use them to create hundreds of small microsites linking to your main web pages with a proper address. It will get your whole site penalised, and possibly cause irrecoverable damage.

Once you've acquired a suitable URLURL it will of course feature throughout your website in various guises and you should promote the **shortest** easiest to remember version wherever you can, so that's on business cards, email footers, and company vehicles for example.

Summary — *Keep it simple, short and local. And purchase the best you can reasonably afford, even if it means paying £200 or so to a cyber-squatter.*

Whilst on the subject of cyber-squatters if you do find yourself considering purchasing a web address from anyone, assuming it's a non-trading business or has virtually no other assets, then as a rule of thumb use the Google keyword tool to estimate all the traffic volume for words that are identical or nearly identical to the name for sale, multiply a year's volume by the cost per click and aim to pay that figure, that is around the value of a year's clicks. In our experience this will rarely be as much as the seller wants but will unusually represent fair value for both sides. Don't include words that are similar but not that similar.

Chapter 20
Which URL? Which is a Good URL – Which is a Great One?

The answer to this topic will vary from time to time as the search engines continually update their algorithms, and sometimes roll them back, like Asda, not that they'll talk about it with quite the same gusto!

If we go back a few years, engines like Google seemed to assume that if you featured a product or service in your URL, let's stick to plumbing, then that's all you did and you would struggle to get found for anything associated, such as Tiling or Air-Conditioning Servicing.

Roll forward a few years and it became essential to have the words describing what you do in your URL, exactly, If you sold Plumbing Tools, you needed to have a URL like www.plumbingtools.co.uk (we actually worked on this one in 2012) to get anywhere.

Things then shifted to the point where having words like plumbing tools would actively **stop** your business being given much priority in this area, but you might do well in related terms relevant to what plumbers do, presumably as Google hoped to nudge businesses towards paid advertising via PPC.

Things are a little more complicated right now, especially within Google and using the above analogy it seems as if you did indeed have plumbing tools in the URL (and content) then you will again gain some prominence for said terms, but if you can make the website more varied with other products and services, the likelihood of doing even better will increase, so counter intuitively to what you might expect. In essence, the more you can muddy water to suggest you are not that interested in a particular niche, the more Google will reward you in that niche!

Particularly with the advent of mobile, searches on the go are important and the search engines try and accommodate an element of accurate regionalism into the results where possible, so it makes sense to accommodate this where possible, and the 2018 roll-out of the Google First mobile algorithm means having your web's presence mobile friendly should be an absolute priority.

The other major point about names and web searches is that when a business starts out online it can expect the vast majority of searchers to find it (and seek it out) using words that describe what the business **does**, not who it **is**. In the case of Plumbers in Northampton that's what people would search for, not Joe himself. Over time, this changes and as people become familiar with a business the proportion searching for you by name (business name not literally your name unless that's the same thing!) will increase and become the largest proportion of web traffic. Using consumer goods as an example, in the early years Dyson may have been discovered by accident when people searched for cleaners or vacuums, now people would be comfortable searching on Dyson.

Summary – *Keep the URL short and descriptive, and local if possible and please ensure everything is mobile friendly.*

Chapter 21
The Importance of Good Ancestors (& History)

When you buy your URL (from a reputable supplier in your target country) it makes sense to check if it has been used before as just like cars, they can have prior crash damage and have effectively been written off – in our world that means they were banned or penalised.

The same applies when buying a business which already has a URL. Don't forget to consider its past history online as even if the current website stats look good it could be a website in decline with trends on the way down in a market that is otherwise very buoyant, so your new business is in fact already being penalised. This could even be the case if the site traffic is flat, for example, in a market that is growing.

Seemingly new and unused web address should generally be trouble free as any bad marks associated with past behaviours, irrespective of whether they were intentional or unintentional, should be wiped clean by the search engines once they see a web address is no longer being used. But as it can take many months for a little used web address to get spidered by the engines' automated algorithms (and who knows how long they keep bad history records for) so we say, why take the chance?

The easiest way to check if a site has existed before, even if nothing appears live now, is to check out the Wayback Machine at https://archive.org/ . If there is no prior history for your intended URL, then you are safe to buy. If it has been used by a previous owner online in the last couple of years, get a reputable online marketing agency to check it out for you to see if it's good history or bad.

Using PlumbingTools as our example again, as you can see below, we were pretty safe to resurrect a site in 2012 and when the original site was built in 2008 it was a virgin unused URL and therefore safe.

Summary of plumbingtools.co.uk

You are probably wondering at this point what makes history so important and what can go wrong?

Within the 140 or so factors that impact a website's potential prominence within the search engine results, the search engine algorithms appear to treat prior history particularly seriously – presumably as there is a perception that an old site that has been regularly updated is likely to be credible and therefore serving it up as an answer to a search query is likely to win favour with more internet users than a new site with little credibility?

In addition to this the engines have realised that other people talking about, referencing and even linking to and from a website is a vote of confidence, so from this have created the concept of bad neighbourhoods. In just the same way that troublesome people tend to group together on an estate, the engines assume if you are associated with a dodgy site, or even a slightly dodgy web-developer, then chances are you are dodgy too. This will mark down your chances of success online so if a website URL has been used before you need to be mindful it could have a good or bad history due to mixing in bad company.

Anything linking to pornography, adult services, gambling or high pressure sales areas like ambulance chasing lawyers, double glazing, solar panels and the like are therefore best avoided.

Summary – *Try and find a new unused URL or one that's been dormant for at least a couple of years. If you are acquiring a business, get a professional to check out for links to and from bad neighbourhoods. It's also a good idea to try and identify sources of regular visitors (using tools like Alexa) to check if the URL is associated with spammy countries such as India.*

Chapter 22
Don't be Two-Faced!

Obviously this is good advice in any social context, whether business or personal, it's also of interest in a website context!

We have no idea why it happens but depending upon whom you choose to buy your URL from, the supplier, without being asked, may set you up at the outset and with no extra cost, with both a WWW and a HTTP version of your website. They probably do it to be helpful!

There is really no need for two types of URL as WWW before a URL automatically alerts the computer server that you are seeking a website using the HTTP data protocol, and HTTP before a URL also confirms you are using the HTTP protocol. However, to Google this looks like you have intentionally set up two distinct faces for your website, a WWW version and a HTTP version, and as they are identical it appears as if you are playing tricks (like creating landing pages or microsites) to get more traffic to your site by having multiple ways in, that is you hope to score more than one result in a search enquiry thereby blocking out your competitors and gaining a larger proportion of the traffic.

You didn't intentionally play a trick on the search engines but they will penalise you from the outset (well, as soon as they spot it) just as if you had done so. Back to our plumbing analogy, the same "dodgy" approach would be to have a main website at plumbingtools.co.uk but also to have built a website on plumbingtoolsnorthampton.co.uk and joesplumbing.co.uk and linked them all to the main plumbingtools.co.uk site.

This was a valid strategy many years ago but creating multiple sites will **always** result in the search engines penalising one or all of your sites (which means they won't get positively promoted) and at worst you can get banned altogether with your site removed from the index (which means you become invisible and can't be found in search enquiries – so the only visitors your site will receive will be those typing the full web address into their browser, not via a search engine).

Summary – *Check that you won't unintentionally have multiple versions of your website seemingly live. Users of older versions of Magento e-commerce software can also sometimes experience a similar problem in that to be helpful the system creates multiple versions of pages, which can confuse the search engines even though it presumably speeds up performance for users of the affected site.*

Chapter 23
Straplines and Your USP

It could of course be argued that we are drifting more into general marketing advice here by commenting on things like straplines and Unique Selling Propositions, but in fact it has a surprising impact on businesses' online performance in ways you probably wouldn't expect.

Let's set the scene first and remember that for most businesses, Google drives the bulk of traffic, or at least it does amongst those with a mind-set to transact as distinct from those say wanting to blog or digest information. Sites like eBay and Amazon are of course big drivers of commerce but in the main this impacts more heavily in a B2C (business to consumer) context so is relevant to those with physical products to sell online rather than say services.

So, accepting that Google is important (and we estimate prominence on this channel alone will more than double almost any business's market share) it's vital not to do anything that will upset them – one thing that does this is when searchers on the search engine bounce straight back out and do a new search.

This so-called Bounce Rate is the length of time before a visitor bounces back out of whichever page they were led to (so often the Home Page) and if it is too short, that is quick, they assume you didn't like the presented content and felt the need to search again. And this worries the search engines, as if it happens too frequently, wouldn't you switch to a better performing search engine? They react by penalising the sites and pages with the worst bounce rates.

And you've probably guessed the end of this story. One way to help encourage people to stay just a little longer on your website pages (and we are talking seconds and fractions of seconds here, not necessarily minutes) is by ensuring you have a good strapline so you immediately alert people what your business does and why it is good versus your competitors.

Using Joe's Plumbers again as our example, underneath their logo it might be an idea to feature something like "Your Local Fast & Tidy Plumbers".

Having a unique proposition is of course important in any business and whilst it is rare to find a truly unique offering (isn't everything a copy of something else these days?) it is important to hone down as much as possible to identify which niche offering you can service with the nearest thing to a unique benefit versus your competition.

Then with a USP worked out it is a great idea to try and work a unique benefit into every page of your website, even down at product level. This means no two pages will have exactly the same content or meta data, and if you can regularly refresh the content, so much the better as gone are the days when search engines expected you to upload content once and leave it unchanged forever (to save them money) – these days they can cope with the costs of change and as a result they actively seek it out and businesses offering the best content will tend to thrive more than others.

The latest changes in Google are also extending the amount of content that can be listed in meta-description which is increasing to 300 characters or so in 2018. It's important to stand out by using this extra capability as we believe they will eventually penalise those with less content (all part of a plan to push results down the page even more and stimulate advertising as an alternative).

Summary – *Identify what you are good at, then make sure the world knows, and keep reinforcing this in different ways throughout your site. Think of it like creating lots of mini-adverts in the newspapers!*

Chapter 24
Building an Online Family Tree

This is something of a contentious area amongst Online Marketers and we even have differing views within my own agency about the extent to which you should build your website or online presence around the words and phrases that people are actually typing into the Internet as search queries. I will guide you using what we consider to be the prevailing approach at the moment, but this will change, so beware following it too slavishly.

Any business area can have thousands of potential keywords that could drive a relevant audience into the spider's web of content you call your online presence, irrespective of whether it's a traditional brochure website, a full e-commerce site, a social presence or something else.

Some of these words or phrases will be high level category killer terms – so things like *plumber* or *jewellers* or in our case *SEO*. Any business dominating these terms consistently will be getting huge amounts of web traffic but also probably a higher bounce rate and not necessarily the best conversion figures as the terms themselves are simply so broad.

Then we can drill down into still very important terms but reaching a slightly more discerning audience from say those simply researching an area for a project. So we might have *Bathroom Plumber*, *Wedding Jewellers* or *SEO Agency* as next level phrases. By now you can feel that we are getting ever closer to an audience with a proposed transaction in mind – they have a bathroom to plumb, are getting married or need an online agency, hopefully not all at once or said new bathroom would become very crowded!

We can, as we have alluded to previously, then drill even further by adding in a regional or demographic focus. This might prompt terms such as *Female Bathroom Plumber*, *Asian Wedding Jewellers* and *SEO Agency Northants* as possible extensions, some of which will be valid searched terms attracting traffic, others might not be exact and the words need experimenting with so perhaps swapping the word Female for Lady, Jewellers for Jewellery and SEO for Optimisation or Optimization depending on whether you can spell or not!

By using keyword tools to estimate the traffic for all the most relevant terms within a particular market it is then possible to group them according to silos, that is bringing together terms with a similar theme, and those with similarly large monthly traffic estimates albeit different themes.

By arranging these in a family tree or pyramid type structure it is possible to create a visual map of all the search terms you want to target as the primary part of your campaign and these may be used as the navigation structure, page content and links around your website.

Using Plumbing Tools as our example again, we would arrive at a potential structure as follows:

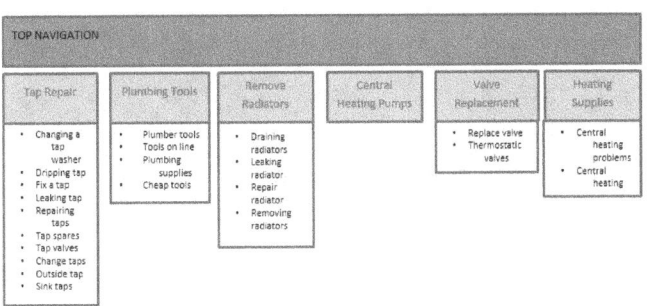

NB. This differs slightly from the live site which still has some additional pages live, for example Leaking Taps & Leaking Tap, this was an acceptable SEO strategy some years ago with each page matching exactly a search term suggested by Google, whereas now at the time of writing the search engines are smart enough to deduce the topic is essentially the same so any superfluous page is seen as playing a trick. This can of course be argued across all of this content as it is all describing similar plumbing problems and solutions, but for the sake of explaining the point, we have let this chart through! The key is to ensure your content is unique, interesting and as informative as possible with as few overlaps across your site sections.

Summary – *Clearly understand what problems your business solves and write as much unique content as possible, drilling down if you can into sensible niches, and place these within your website in silos and categories of related information to help give the search engines a greater clue as to the overall theme in that part of the site. In this way you can build your profile as an Information destination site, worthy of merit.*

Chapter 25
Key Website Functionality

A website does of course need a lot more than some unique content and pictures to make it relevant, interesting and of course usable to your intended audience. With circa 140 factors influencing how the search engines rate and then rank your content, it is of no surprise that a number of factors make it on to the top of our list as priorities.

We have talked already about different types of websites needing clever edit engines for publishing content in a nice format. In bigger businesses this extends to giving content writers rights to edit and rights to publish, plus a possibility of having senior editors with different rights, so for this some form of Content Management System is needed.

For e-commerce businesses there needs to be an ability to publish product data, specific meta-data and descriptions about said products plus useful information at category level, for example Plumbing Tools. There is also a need to take payments, typically via Credit, Debit or Charge Card, via PayPal or in recent times it's relevant to consider recurring payments such as Online Direct Debit, or even Bitcoin payment options. In all cases it is then necessary to have an interface with a Bank (so you can access the money in the real world) and to facilitate this it is often necessary to have a relationship with a Payment Services Provider or Merchant Acquirer. These middle men are often owned by the Banks and big examples include Barclaycard, WorldPay, First Data and of course American Express and PayPal, the latter being both payment choice and scheme operator, just to add to the confusion!

Beyond this list of key functionality it is currently important for your web presence to have:

An easily accessible and direct link to your social channels, better still if it's in a highly visible part of the website quickly observed by the search engine robots, such as the masthead (top) rather than hidden at the foot of the site. This is still a common mistake.

Easily readable (so not an image) contact and address details, so the search engines can better understand where you operate. And if you have more than one location, list them. If they have the ability to receive post this opens up an opportunity to get listed by the engines for each location – but they will check each out that it is a proper address.

About Us content that explains the rationale for your business.

A sitemap (two versions), one for humans, the other for search engine robots to help them navigate their way around your content. Even better if this is automatically updated by your site platform every time the site itself is edited.

Terms & Conditions and a Privacy Policy. These may be tedious but some engines look for this content as evidence that businesses are using good practice and trading ethically, so why not include it. Lawyers can help prepare this if you don't have it. As an alternative if budgets are tight read a few of your competitors' examples and rewrite a new version of your own, but don't be tempted to copy word for word. If you do go the D-I-Y approach, understand it may expose your business to commercial risk versus a properly constructed paid for version!

News or a blog, preferably hosted on your own site (rather than linking out to blogger software and giving the brownie points to them). This is a great way of making your web content appear fresh and newsworthy and this is what the search engines tend to prefer now that data storage costs have dropped so much — whereas in the past they preferred well written unchanging content. Even better if you can have a data feed from your news onto some of the harder to update pages of your site where content rarely changes, such as key category pages. This will make it appear as if that page is also regularly updating.

Similar in purpose to news or blogs are having Articles and White Papers on your site. These represent an opportunity for your business to express a passionate and often controversial view on a particular topic, and this will encourage word-of-mouth referral, make your site look newsworthy and gain you the moral high-ground as an industry spokesman. Carefully structured topics also enable you to widen the breadth of keywords that your web presence can become associated with as an expert or destination site. So the more you can say, the better.

Pages specific to your own business or industry — in the case of Plumbing Tools they have some brand names unique to them such as Radclamp and Pozibite, plus a business name Advanced Building Design, (which offers a broader range than just plumbing), so each of which will merit some dedicated content.

Add all this together and you can see how what started life as a seemingly simple website idea might now feature content organised something like this, not one page but 50 or so, all unique and focussed so as to be most visible and attractive to the search engines.

In simple terms, the more boring the content, put it at the bottom, the more relevant and interesting, near the top so it's where prospective customers' eyes will go first.

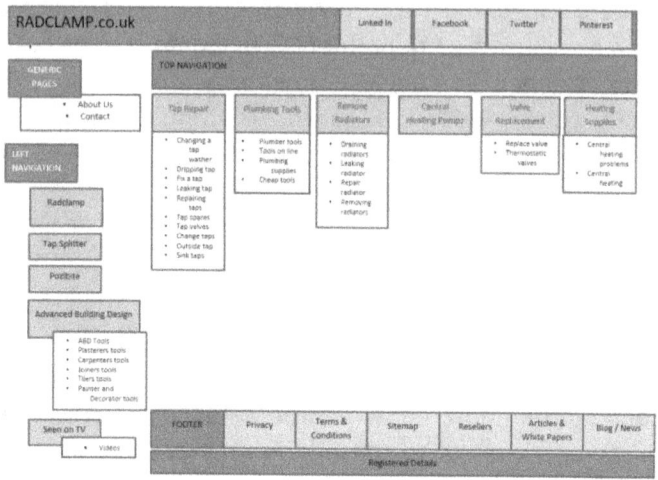

When structuring your website it is of course vital to consider it will be visited by real people and however they behave will be observed by the search engines, so for example if they bounce straight back out again into the search engine it's not rocket science to deduce the content was either irrelevant to the search term used, or the website is hard to use, or maybe the products aren't priced attractively.

Over time if enough people exhibit the same behaviour, the engines will form a pretty robust opinion of which of these factors applies to which page, and they will reward or penalise your web page accordingly as they don't ever want to serve bad results which make them look bad.

It is therefore absolutely vital to ensure your web content has all the required capabilities relevant to your business, that they work and are easy to use, so put yourself in your customers' shoes and try them yourselves.

As mentioned a high bounce rate is indicative of a problem and whilst not always achievable depending on sector and type of web presence, aim for less than 25% bouncing out quickly within 5 seconds or less.

We have always found it very useful to consider Thinking Styles or Cognitive Styles www.how-to-study.com/mobile/article.asp?id=198 when creating a roadmap for your online content and which functions are key within, say, your website. Taking it a stage further some people will be driven by strong visuals, others seek lots of supporting information, and others regard reviews as important.

Imagine your business sells televisions, it's not unreasonable to expect that some prospects know precisely they want a Sony XYZ 123 model, others might just want a Sony, some will just be searching out televisions and others could just be killing a few spare minutes online during their lunch break looking for inspiration or bargains – so not distinct from browsing the Boxing Day Sales.

If your website is built with the key functions necessary to display, say, sale items, strong visuals, lots of supporting lists of features, reviews and all backed by a capable search function on site that can cope with multiple words leading to one product, you are half way there. A good membership and checkout and payment system completes the picture.

In this scenario all that then matters re additional key functionality is how easy is it for you the administrator, or your team, to run the online site and update content, pictures, prices, plus of course compile databases of customer queries, comments, orders etc. Such data needs to feed easily out to picking and packing in the warehouse or reporting into the marketing team (for repeat communications) or accounts team so you can pay your taxes! Get this key functionality wrong and you will have a difficult to run online business, get it right and it may almost run itself.

Summary – *Ensure you have all the key functional areas covered and ensure you have no dead-ends: everything needs to link somewhere.*

It's easy to build all your key functionality around the potential customer, and that's no bad thing, but do remember you need to be able to run the business easily and cost effectively too. In our experience just 20 e-commerce sales a day can break a business's backbone due to time inefficiencies – go above this and systems need consideration to help.

Chapter 26
No Cheating

Imitation is not the sincerest form of flattery or is it?

Imitation may be appreciated in real-life, but online it's not, at least not where the search engines are concerned. In general terms they DO like it if one person or another (and by person we really mean web page) talks about or references another's content, so you might recommend what you have found elsewhere, you might write a short precis or even link to it. They regard this as a vote of confidence and that's one of many ways they can determine what's hot to trot and what's not.

In Google's case they have a concept called PageRank™ https://en.wikipedia.org/wiki/PageRank named after one of the founders, that uses these votes to estimate the relative importance of one page of content online versus another and this in turn is used as a significant ranking factor in determining the SERPS or search engines positions for said content.

As you might imagine, such an important element has been reverse engineered to the nth degree and tinkered with to spoof the search engine algorithms, leading to businesses swapping and trading links with one another, in an attempt to game the system. Whilst PageRank™ scores aren't officially published by Google any more the gaming continues and probably will forever. It's not a strategy we condone if you want reliable long-term success for your online pages and online business.

A better approach is to ensure your online pages are full of unique content, written with a genuine audience in mind. This means you have to fight the urge to ever copy anything you see on any other website, never lift their text and re-use it, don't even copy their navigation if you can avoid it – this is for the simple reason that they may be being penalised, or about to be due to dodgy practices which look good right now but won't work forever.

It's fine to read other online content, get a feel for it and then rewrite it using your own style and words, and this needs doing for as much of your site as possible. The content also needs to be regularly updated, not posted and forgotten – unless it's an archive or blog quickly replaced with something newer.

Creating unique content extends to avoiding the temptation to try and overuse or keyword-stuff those words or phrases you want to target. Just talk naturally and let the search engine algorithms work out the rest.

You can use http://www.copyscape.com/ to check if any content is unique or your content is being re-used, if it is, you will lose out particularly if the offender had their version observed by the search engines before yours was picked up. Send them a strongly worded letter asking for it to be changed.

Summary – *In short, if you think you've come across a good wheeze to cheat and speed up this online malarkey, such as copying other people's sites or content, don't!*

Chapter 27
The Importance of Uniqueness and Good Content

We keep hammering on about good and unique content, but what exactly is that?

You could write the world's most informative piece of prose about your chosen subject but it still may not be good enough for the search engines. And that might be for a number of reasons.

First off, and least likely, is the point alluded to in the previous section: your content could have been syndicated out and noticed first by a more established website than yours (it could still be from an inferior, smaller or newer business, just a better optimised one) that is copying you. This could be fraudulent if they are lifting your content without permission (so always ensure your website carries a copyright provision in its terms and conditions) or unintentional.

For example you may create great content, send it out to your business partners who are pleased to feature it, but they have better and more established websites higher up the search engine radar. So their version gets spidered and noticed before you, and they are hence generally attributed as the editor and originator – then when your version gets found on your site, you are conceptually marked down as a me-too copy, and hence awarded few if any brownie points for your troubles. It may not be fair, but that's how it works.

- Your content isn't unique, it has too many sentences similar to others online. Copyscape is the route to check for this.

- The content doesn't fulfil a real need – so nobody bothers to stay and read it for long or recommend it

OK, your content is good, you're first to market, but is it good enough?

These days to be classed as good content, and by that we mean for the search engines to bother keeping a copy in their main index, studying it fully, and ranking it, all of which costs them money, then ideally you also need to address the following:

- Be unique as mentioned already and answer a question if you possibly can, so, as an example, "How to Pick a Good SEO Agency?"
- Target a niche audience with a problem
- Ensure the tech is correct – so good use of Meta and any mark-up languages currently required by the engines. Complete as many fields as possible in your content management system but don't be tempted to just stuff in keywords
- Feature images – again with appropriate tags – and make them interesting
- Consider an Infographic as a better way of stimulating readership and recommendation from others. See the example below – it's just a way of bringing words and data to life through pictures and charts.

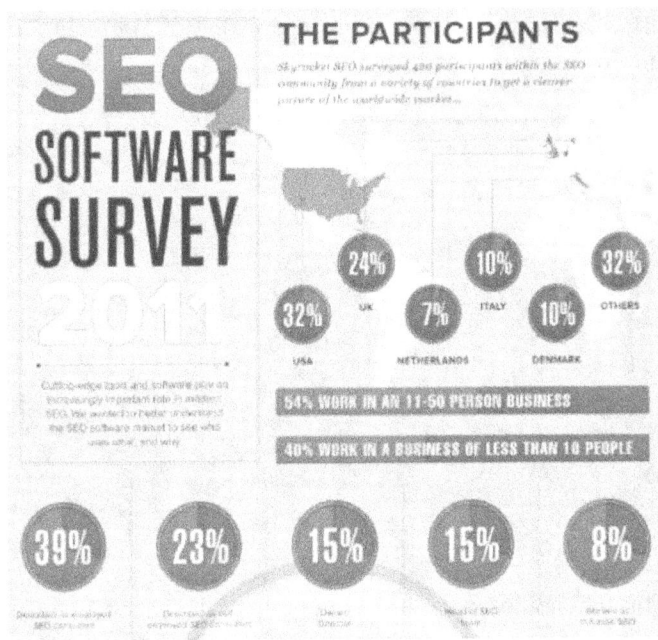

Image from Skyrocket

Infographics are time consuming to create but going back again to our point about different people behaving in different ways, having a visual style will attract people and keep them reading for longer. A tool like Piktochart makes it easier and quicker to create this kind of content.

Not a phrase we particularly like but the concept of creating Link Bait (content people love so much they want to link to it from their own site) is worth taking time to understand. As an example a water business created this infographic which encouraged others to link to it (as it was useful content) and this made the recommended business look good, plus created useful links for Google to follow – so the water site's profile online rose dramatically and with little extra effort. The trick is in thinking of interesting or unique infographic topics.

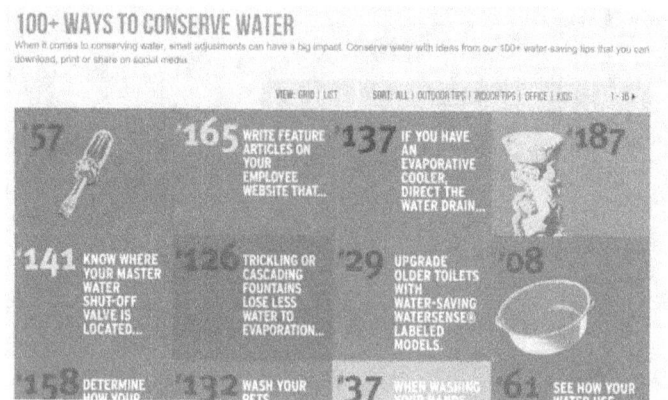

This whole idea is easier to understand if you are a regular reader of news on social media. How often have you been hooked to follow a headline such as, "She gave away her lunch money, you won't believe what happened next." It's a similar concept of drawing people in.

Summary *– Make sure your content is unique, presented in a technically optimal manner, and is compelling to a specific audience. In fact so compelling they recommend it to others.*

Chapter 28
The Basics – Meta, Images, Content

Ok, so you've decided a web site is the right way forward and now have a pretty good idea about the site structure and navigational flow (also called Customer Journey) that you want to impose on your prospects, and you've also decided on core functional needs such as an editorial approval and CMS system, and shopping basket. That must be it, surely, well other than a nice design?

Sadly not. It's important to understand that clever as the modern search engines are, and they are VERY clever, it's actually machines that will, in the main, *read* your website, and a bit like bees, take it back to the nest to be checked over by the Queen, aka, Google or other engines' algorithms which give a page score and hence create a ranking.

In the early days of Search Engine Marketing the engines couldn't read all the content, for example PDFs were deemed too difficult and data intensive to be bothered with, likewise images are a nightmare with a whole set of different attributes. These days it is our belief, even if the engines claim not to be able or claim not to read a particular type of content or code, then they probably can. In fact we'd go further, tests on items explicitly flagged as "nothing to see here, don't even bother looking as we don't want it used to assess our site" have suggested the engines can't resist a sneaky peak.

Whatever you do on your site, be it in the intentional, visible content meant for customers and prospects or the hidden meta-data and code flagged only for computers and browsers to read, it all needs to be of the highest standard, designed to serve a purpose and give a good customer experience, and in no way trying to hoodwink anyone or cut corners.

In the heading to this section we have listed out Meta, images and content. We could also add sitemaps and schema mark up so let's describe those in a little more detail.

Meta-data is hidden content that guides the search engines as to the content of a specific page or area of your site, like a dictionary, and comprises a list of keywords, a short and long description, that is Meta Keywords, Meta Title and Meta Description. The data isn't used in the same way by every engine but it's good practice to fill in as many fields as possible with unique information, and by that we mean unique versus competitors' and also with as few duplications as possible within your own site.

Think of this as an opportunity to hone in on the most relevant keywords that apply to that product or service page and don't be tempted to stuff in too many variances or options – it will look like spam and get you penalised.

The descriptions should generally be as short as possible, and feature a unique selling point, so write them like an advert and with a potential customer in mind, and include important options like Free Delivery rather than using up your keyword limit on repeating your business's brand name and URL, which they already know. If you must put your name, try and leave it to last and ensure the Meta-Title is under 60 characters long or it will be truncated. For meta description we tend to stay under 300 characters long (formerly 150) but many agencies add more. We argue why risk it? You can read more detail on these important topics at:

https://moz.com/learn/seo/title-tag

https://moz.com/learn/seo/meta-description

Images are increasingly important and engines like Google keep developing improved technology in this area, so it's more important than ever to ensure every image is of the highest quality but smallest size possible, and they should be clearly tagged with appropriate keywords – these may be used by screen-readers for blind viewers, and they are also read by the search engines' programs, so take time to make them as relevant and descriptive as possible. Use JPEG format for your photographs and colourful images, use the compressed PNG format for anything else to help speed up your site download speeds and impress the search engines.

Sitemaps (mentioned previously as an important website guide to computer and human) need to be created in the appropriate format and kept as up to date as possible, so that's HTML and XML.

Schema Mark-Up is one of the more recent and important elements – similar to image tags, it is a way of adding short tags to pages to help all the main search engines deduce with greater certainty what a page purports to be about – they normally try and estimate this themselves using semantic engines as they can't always trust site owners to tell the truth! By getting the site owner to do this relatively new thing they presumably have concluded the cost saving on processing power for the search engines outweighs the danger of gaming the system – so it's important right now but we expect this to be downgraded in future. Schema.org is a collaboration between Google, Bing, Yandex and Yahoo, so it could be argued it reduces the USP between engines, so that combined with overuse will we believe see this tactic decline in importance over the next few years.

Summary *– Put as much effort into the behind the scenes content and code as you do into the visible bits of* *your website and don't be tempted to cheat by cutting corners or copying. One thing to watch out for are website platforms that automate the creation of content. This is good if it's for an updated sitemap but generally bad if it relates to Meta-Data which needs to vary throughout the site.*

If all your site is out of date and you are daunted by having so much to change, start with every new page or product you add, then tackle things one category at a time. Even if it takes six months to get everything right it's preferable to doing nothing.

Chapter 29
Remember to be Sales Focused

We have hinted at this previously re Meta-Data but as it's important to the success of any web business, irrespective of the channel or means through which you intend to deliver your message, we will labour the point.

Your content needs to be unique, written for a prospect in mind (and like all good marketing offers a user benefit not just a product feature) and it needs to be written in a way that is compelling to close a sale, or whatever counts for success in your business, such as a sign-up, or membership.

Approach your content like a salesperson and ensure as often as possible you include calls to action, a reason for people to want to buy and the means for them to do so.

In simple terms then use things like *Free Delivery, Buy 1, Get 1 Half price, Offer closes in 3 hours, Only 47 memberships left* or whatever works best for you, and do so wherever you can. Ensure your content feels like an informative advert not a staid brochure. If you ask people to respond and give them the means to do so, they often will, but if you create unnecessary barriers or fail to sell the sizzle of your business, few will struggle on for you.

Summary – *Buy a great book like Ogilvy on Advertising to learn more about how people respond, and incorporate interesting benefits to make people buy wherever you can.*

Chapter 30
Be Sociable Even If You Hate It

In the next section, *Be Sociable Even If You Hate It*, I tackle the practical ways of developing your online presence in social media..

For many people this is a necessary evil, but if you follow my advice and focus on what can make you successful, I think I can minimise the pain and really increase your marketing presence.

There is a mind-set shift at the heart of this – and I've seen the pain it can cause people, almost regardless of age – but with our years of experience, built up at the same time as the presence of social media has grown, we can provide you not only with the practical insights and tools and actions, but also help motivate you to get cracking and be more successful than your competitors.

Section 4
Be Sociable – Even If You Hate It

Chapter 31
Be Sociable – but Keep Your Business and Private Lives Separate

OK, you've now got your strategy and products sorted, you know who you want to target with your message and you've created a well-structured web presence to engage people. Surely you don't need to be sociable too?

Unfortunately, you do as having a noticeably popular social presence will generally improve your search engine rankings as it influences the search engine algorithms more and more, and of course you may also get some direct custom via the social media channels themselves, that is prospects finding you without using a search engine. Whatever next!

A strange quirk of the online marketing world in recent years, and you may be questioning why, is the seemingly endless march of social channels and the increasingly important part they play in our lives and commerce generally – in short, we believe you can blame Google.

Consider for a moment if some years ago Google in its wisdom had declared that any social platform was its commercial enemy (as it is potentially a competitor for our time and eye-balls and hence targets many of the same advertisers as Google itself), so, within their algorithms they would have marked down any web presence that had a strong social presence or links off the site to easily enable social sharing. In the early days this was easily detectable, not least because to a limited degree the companies collaborated on friendly terms with Google. If they'd made that kind of announcement way back when, then SEO companies around the world would have spread the word and eventually almost every web developer would be advising their clients: "No, you don't need one of those social things, it will harm your online business." End of problem.

Now the social networks would of course probably still exist but in our view they wouldn't be anywhere near as prevalent as at present nor have the huge pull on people's time. Today, in almost every major company they now have staff dedicated to running social channels, and smaller firms use agencies or the boss does it themselves, even though many hate it and can't really see the point of wasting valuable time on trivialities. I for one have no real passion in showing people what I've just had for dessert and where I had it, in fact the correct answer for Mrs H is of course: "No dear, I certainly didn't have a desert and I'm not a member of their custard reward club."

We should add of course that not all social content needs to be meaningless!

But by making social media an active and growing part of the search engine's algorithm, and this isn't confined to Google, the search engines have in effect added fuel to the fire and helped bolster their enemies and every web developer worth their salt tells clients: "I'm afraid so – you do need one of those social things but don't worry we'll all have fun promoting it, and we can do some lovely expensive-looking graphics for you that will hardly cost a song."

Now, armed with billions of daily *engagements* with users, the social channels are starting to compete effectively as alternative advertising channels to the search engines, hitherto the world's biggest advertisers. Maybe it's poetic justice – and it may change, if we ran Google, at some point in the future we would indeed start to down-play the statistical importance of social signals, not least because now that these mega businesses don't exactly get along so well with each other (as they compete for advertisers' spend), they tend not to share data so readily if at all – so the search engines are now, to an extent, in the dark as to how well your business is really doing socially, which makes it hard for them to rank things well.

But for now that's not the case and your business should generally consider building an effective social presence on the main social networks. For most businesses that means Twitter, for those unlikely to get negative customer feedback it could extend to Facebook, and for those with a very visual element, consider Pinterest. These are currently our channels of choice in this medium.

To some extent we consider reviews, blogs and white-papers or articles as part of the social landscape as they all also have potential to deliver a highly targeted message and get shared, and in the case of reviews delivered through a schema mark-up (so they can be easily read and standardised) these win some favour within the engines' algorithms at present in 2018.

If the business has or is likely to have a significant following then a LinkedIn business profile is worth establishing, or for the business owner and key staff it is also worth considering building a personal profile but consider too that this profile will leave when the staff member leaves the company, and can be damaged if they do anything controversial, so don't put all your eggs in that fragile basket alone!

This controversy extends to the temptation to tag business posts into personal profiles, for example in Facebook, but it really is best keeping work and business separate. I remember fondly the day we discovered a client in the children's market posted pictures on the shared Facebook pages (used for both business and pleasure) of their, let's just say, a*dult* holiday. It was nothing illegal but it certainly wasn't appropriate to share with kids, their mums and dads and the corporate sponsors!

Summary – *Be as sociable as you can but keep business and your private life separate and watch out for trends or news headlines regarding how important this is to the search engine algorithms. It's currently (Q1 2018) a top ten on the* to do *list so I'm afraid all those sceptics out there and old fuddies like me: yes – you do need a social presence, even if you fake an interest!*

Chapter 32
Leveraging Word-of-Mouth

A very common failing of businesses online is to treat the social channels much as they would a newswire or PR service: they simply blast out news about the latest client wins, or promote the same old boring promotional features of their product every day, just rotating the message a little bit every few weeks. Its looks stale, it is stale, and it will come as no surprise that prospective *users* of said content become about as quickly bored of the content even if they work in the sector. In fact they are just as bored as the poor staff creating the content under a three-line-whip from the boss to *do something* everything day. This is not the way to win friends and influence people socially or at dinner parties.

The secret of good social is to imagine it more as a two way conversation – sure you will have things to say about the company, its products, latest widget invention or colour scheme, new offers and client signings, but you'll also a view on *some* topics happening in the broader world, and you'll want to engage in a bit of back and forth dialogue with your clients and prospects, if at all possible.

In short it doesn't look like a forum for a megaphone blasting out the same stuff every day or week.

Now notice here we said *some* topics. If you are in the lingerie market it may be entirely acceptable to comment on the latest celebrity b**b job, if you are a business consultant, less so. Ditto things like politics. It's very hard to know people's views even if they are your customers so by all means comment on things like the latest data on savings or interest rates but pcrhaps best to avoid being too specific in areas like sex, gender, politics, religion,

Brexit. You get the idea – plus of course every industry has its own contentious areas so you could either avoid these or make them an area for comment where you aim to be seen taking the moral high-ground and becoming seen as a regular commentator and source of good information.

This of course takes some of the fun out of social media by removing the chance to respond to hate mail, but trust us, it's for the best. It does make it harder though to think up interesting content that has the potential to engage people. And this is where tactics like competitions, giveaways, infographics, surveys and link-bait and awards come into their own. We've talked a little about some of these but let's expand here how they can be used strategically.

Running competitions and providing giveaways are fairly obvious. Simply have an idea, provide some kind of prize or offer and feature it online plus use your email database if appropriate to spread the word. Contrary to what you would think if you read the rules of other businesses' promotions, (you do need rules) it is generally acceptable to offer cash as a prize, and if you are clever with your terms and conditions and small-print you can run multiple draws across say a year, each featuring the same core prize fund but showing different pictures representing what the cash could be spent on: a car in one, a holiday in another, for example. So don't let cost put you off being creative beyond giving away the latest iPad.

PS. An important element is that generally everyone should have the same chance of winning and they shouldn't need to pay to enter, or you may be running an illegal lottery. You can find more about this kind of thing by researching Sales Promotion Law.

Infographics are of course a great way of visually bringing information to life or telling a story and encouraging people to share the information. Along with simple surveys they are one of the best ways of spreading the word and again needn't cost a fortune to create or administer, if you shop around – and even old boring stories from years ago can be livened up and retold with nice graphics and a good flow chart as it makes the boring more accessible and understandable.

We have alluded already to how a strong and intriguing question can be used to hook people into clicking on a first page and then going further (click-bait). Well this concept can be taken further if you encourage people to put a summary about your information on their own site (as they need content too, many will oblige) plus a link to your full content (link-bait). This all adds up to something the search engines like to see as it looks like genuine interest.

One of the most ambitious ways to spread word about your business is to create your own Annual Awards. Pick a number of ideal potential winners and communicate to them that they are on the short-list (that you invented, preferably with at least one partner in crime), and encourage links from their heavily trafficked sites to your award pages which have been especially created for the promotion. Many businesses, even large ones, will be chuffed to bits to think they have been specially selected and are seen as worthy of praise – it's not so different from winning a star from the teacher at school. On the special web pages created, you can of course welcome further entries from other companies too.

Creating an award like this has many benefits ranging from getting your name out there into your target clients' businesses (where it may be internally spread around), enabling your business to be seen to take the high ground in a market space and USP niche of **exactly** your choosing, making your business look bigger and more impressive, and it will give you lots to talk about socially. The links back will also generally help your natural search engine rankings improve, so it's a win-win, provided it's implemented properly and with professionalism, plus of course it has to be for a sensible and serious purpose.

Summary – *Stick to content that's at least half appropriate to your audience but don't be afraid to experiment with consumer type activities to get people engaged at a deeper level.*

Chapter 33
Don't Be Too Sociable and Don't Let Just Anyone Do It for You

It's easy to assume from this that all social content must be good and the more you do the better?

Wrong.

Some years ago we came across a company with circa 200 staff that understandably felt they had some catching up to do socially, as they hadn't done much, so they gave all their employees **free rein** to do pretty much whatever they liked on any social network to promote the business or activities of the staff, and they could each do it for **30 minutes** a day at the company's expense.

So that's 100 hours of social activity a day, circa 25,000 hours per year – if they tried to do that much through an agency it could easily add up to £1m a year budget. So that must be great, surely?

Actually it wasn't.

It didn't work for several reasons.

Firstly there was a lot of overlap and confusion, secondly a lot of the content was inappropriate for a business trying to build a credible brand they were proud of, plus of course novices would create output that just wouldn't get any traction with a broader audience, influencers or even the search engines.

And the final nail in the coffin was that the opportunity cost of these staff if they had used that half hour on income earning activities for their own business was actually over £2m, so they were wasting money in the search for something free.

The correct social strategy for this business may have been no more than around 20 hours of work per month but deployed in strategically important places so it was more likely to be picked up in the right places and shared appropriately. This might have cost say £20k per annum to outsource to a good supplier, a lot of money but only 1% of the value wasted by being too sociable in the wrong places. In short, they could have saved 99% by spending 1%. It's food for thought and whilst not a common case, most businesses are guilty of similar actions, albeit unintentionally, including ours! (One example that springs to mind is that we sometimes have a go at design or updating our own IT infrastructure.)

Another common area of mistake is to create a bunch of content – so maybe white-papers or articles or thought provoking topics and then blast the same communication out through every channel such as Facebook, Twitter, LinkedIn in the assumption that each of these audiences will be pleased at the originality and not see the other channels with the same content at the same time. It is vitally important to remember that each marketing channel does NOT have an exclusive clientele. Your own prospects and clients will access news about your business through multiple means online and offline, and over a prolonged period, so if you put the same content out through each possible channel at the same time, they will notice, they will be bored, they might even be annoyed.

It is better to be a little antisocial and pump out less content on each channel but do your very best to make it unique to each or with a slight different flavour to suit potentially different demographics of each channel.

Summary – *Better to do a small amount of the right strategic things than too much of the tactical things, which* *will waste effort and indirectly money. And try and keep all channels a little bit different to engage people who've probably already seen your message elsewhere. They may realise its familiar but won't get annoyed if they recognise you at least made an effort at varying things, so that applies to headings and images as well as content.*

Chapter 34
Friends in Only the Right Places

When creating your web content, whether it's a website, social pages or blog, it is of course important to interact with other people or businesses in as natural a way as possible – we talk more on this subject in a minute in a concept you may have heard of called *Bad Neighbourhoods* (or *Neighborhoods* if you spell it incorrectly in certain parts of the globe with slightly eccentric Presidents).

A key point here is the word *natural*. This is important because firstly you will potentially upset and drive away your genuine prospective customers if your online presence doesn't feel right, it looks too contrived, is trying too hard or has too many of a particular thing (links, reviews, adverts for example) and secondly, the search engines themselves are using automated tools to measure what seems *natural* to them, both through a simple count of these attributes on each page and also through any metrics they can detect from said page that reflect consumer behaviour, so things like Bounce Rate (how quickly they leave), Dwell Time (obviously that's time on page), Session Time (and number of pages viewed in total). All combined with Entry and Exit points as well.

The search engines are also good at looking at Trend data, so a sudden influx of more of something (links, reviews, pages to name just a few) has the potential to be seen as positive, that is, your site is being updated or has suddenly become newsworthy like Trump's latest pronouncement, or they could think you are playing tricks – in which case you get held back, penalised or banned.

What you are aiming for is a page of content that seems to be in accord with what you might obviously expect, so yet another reason to try and avoid tricks and gaming the system too much. Any content that has zero interaction with other people or content will generally seem a little suspect, not least because it is harder to find and if it is in effect a dead-end (stopping the natural flow of surfing around the Internet), and then it's not going to do your business any favours and you should avoid this if you can.

It's really to be commended if you can somehow associate yourself with high profile, credible sources of knowledge within your specific field of interest. This will vary for every business online but in general terms can be considered as places hard to bribe and influence, so that's typically educational establishments, universities, review bodies, government, charities plus very large brands with a large online presence of their own. To a lesser degree it's good to associate with high profile Bloggers and the like but as these are often know to be susceptible to money through sponsorship, advertising, product placement and the like, view any association as of short term tactical traffic benefit rather than long term and strategic. But these are all good places to associate with and should be encouraged, however difficult and time consuming that is – please do not be tempted to try and do it quickly or cheaply by buying friends in-bulk from offshore!

Summary – *Be sociable with the right kind of informed people and businesses and try and do things that always look and feel natural, preferably with real people and organisations in your home and preferred market, not bought in offshore.*

Chapter 35
Do you want to live in a Bad Neighbourhood?

So what about these *Bad Neighbourhoods* we've been talking about, what are they?

This is a throw-back to the days when a good way to influence search engine prominence was to have lots of links from other sites back to your own site, irrespective of where or whom they were from – this purporting to look like your content must be interesting and popular, hence you'd move up the search engine rankings.

The search engines reacted to this by giving more brownie-points to links from good trusted sites from reputable owners, which is fair enough, and then they reduced the beneficial impact if a site was referring lots of others – in effect diluting the benefit thereby making it harder to spoof and sell this as a means to influence search engines.

The logic behind all this makes perfect sense. Let's say I own a local hairdressers and get a link back from the local plumber – that's entirely logical. If the BBC featured my latest bouffant style that would be even more valuable. But imagine I was a large software company and the search engine algorithms then noticed I was receiving links in from low level local directories, probably offshore, or a link from the local fish and chip shop - this seems a bit less genuine, so that's how they treat it.

This impact of having best, better, worse *neighbours* in turn created a new opportunity – called Google Bowling, and loosely described this is the means to create deliberately bad links to a competitor's website safe in the knowledge that it would do them harm, as described above, and so by inference might do you good and your own site would rise up the rankings, creating more free sales.

The search engines' reaction to this was a little slow but eventually a pattern seemed to form – bad content and links to your site will now only really do you harm if **you** have been instrumental in creating the association, so if they link to you, not so bad, as it's out of your control, but if **you link to them** and they are viewed as dodgy by the search engines, that's very bad for you as you intentionally took this action. Google Bowling doesn't work so well now, if at all, but you really can scupper your own game unintentionally.

Websites about topics like gambling, pornography, payment protection insurance (or whatever the latest scam of the month is) will generally be poorly viewed by the search engine algorithms even if the sites themselves are hugely popular and well known, and other sites that freely associate with said content will themselves be tarred with a bad brush, albeit to a decreasing degree. Together they form a bad neighbourhood. If you unwittingly associate yourself with part of this network, even an outlying part not necessarily the worst part, by inference you will deemed to be associated and your online content will be marked down. When this unfortunate thing happens you will probably still get found in search results, but less often, so you will get less traffic and less sales and it's not simply a quick fix to remove the links, if you can.

So when anyone contacts your business and says something along the lines of "your content looks great for my audience, will you link to me?" (and they will) beware, and that's irrespective if they offer you a link or traffic back in return. They may look fine but they themselves could be part of a bad neighbourhood and be being marked down, which you don't want to catch like a virus.

If you do inadvertently get into such an arrangement it can usually be corrected by removing said connection, if necessary alerting the search engines – but sometimes damage can be almost irreparable or expensive and time consuming to resolve if it's had a very adverse impact so it's a specialist job normally undertaken by specialist SEO agencies who can paper over the defect with high quality output.

To bring this topic right up to date, that is, 2018, we have now seen instances of brand new websites being penalised by the engines (even whilst they were still being built) as the developer themselves had been connected with various ventures in bad neighbourhoods. The new sites affected that were still being built were entirely reputable and had no obvious faults but started life with a negative against them, which they then had to fight against to gain positive presence, so costing time and money, versus the normal battle of just starting at Go, collect £200, with no handicap.

Summary – It's tough online so pick your associations carefully and with suitable due diligence, don't jump in with both feet. Ask around – referrals can be telling.

Chapter 36
Think a Year Ahead so You Don't Need to Rush

Plan ahead – think of a year's online advent calendar, without surprises!

Many businesses start off with good social intentions, creating content for their blog or Facebook and Twitter every few days only to see enthusiasm wane over a few weeks, plus of course the normal day job tasks quickly take over priority again – we've certainly fallen foul of this in our own agency and always put client deadlines ahead of our own, meaning we deliver what we say but fail to market and grow our own business as diligently as we know we should and can do.

This pressure then pushes businesses into cheating or perhaps more accurately, taking shortcuts, so typically the same content is pushed out through every channel meaning many of your customers will get access to repeated messages – boring. But we've already talked about this risk.

Ultimately it leads to big gaps in social activity, and a panic at seasonally important times, when *we need to get this out today* becomes the mantra, to everyone's dismay in the office.

This creates several problems. Firstly, the search engine algorithms are doing their best to look for trends in any channel, and although they can't currently see everything that goes on in many social channels they will notice spikes in referrals to your site and other metrics, so gaps don't always look so good.

Hurried work is also often not great work and it tends to push the social activity away from strategically important goals and messages – these being replaced with generics like *have a great Xmas* which really serves minimal benefit for anyone.

What's the solution?

It's simple really but harder in practice to do well. What we aim to do for all clients, in advance, is create a seasonal content calendar – so we plan well in advance all the messages that will be created at a given point in the year ahead, we research these thoroughly, we actually write the content nearer the time it's due (as events in marketplaces or society generally can over-take the best laid plan and we don't want to waste effort). Content can then often be tweaked with a different spin and used across several clients, improving our agency's bottom-line and client value-for-money whilst still ensuring the content for each is unique.

We look for important (and less important) dates in the annual calendar using tools like:

https://www.daysoftheyear.com/

It's also important to consider dates relative to the company's industry, so for example an IT company might very well be expected to have something interesting to say when it's the anniversary of the PC being invented and my agency got great results by association for a client by simply remembering some anniversaries that Microsoft had forgotten themselves, about Microsoft products!

Around all this activity, some highly topical and relevant, some on the periphery, it's easy to slot in news and events about the business itself. Then, if the worst thing happens, for example you forget to create content or are simply too busy, it's not the end of the world as the calendar will still look pretty full and cared for even without your own specific news.

By having a wide and varied spread of content you will find you easily have enough to create variety across each online channel, look interesting, and most importantly of all engage prospects in more of an interactive dialogue, not a one-way rant of company news only.

Summary – *Plan well ahead but write nearer the time to avoid wasting effort, be prepared to look outside the obvious interest areas nearest your own business.*

Chapter 37
Make Sure You Fire on All Cylinders

We have already alluded several times to the temptation and common practice of taking your website's news and content, and then pushing it out through every channel with minimal changes – so the same inspirational story can be read on the website, in the blog, on Facebook and LinkedIn, and in edited form on Twitter. Many of your audience will subscribe and follow you in several of these channels and how do you think it will make them feel?

Frustrated, bored, and cheated? Yes, all of these and more.

Not surprisingly the answer is to only use the channels you have time for (and or external resource to help) so you can ensure it is done well and frequently, and where possible unique content (or heavily adapted content) should be used on each channel so if a reader accesses it more than once, they still get to learn something new.

Obviously not every channel is viable or sensible for every business, so for example, if you get lots of bad customer reviews like British Gas or BT, there is a strong argument to avoid said channels and push dialogue with customers through controllable, private routes like email or telephone. This is for the simple reason you don't want existing clients to put off new ones or upset the general mood and brand efforts. Channels like Pinterest enable a more one-sided dialogue from the brand, not the customer.

But if your business can sensibly and usefully use several of the online channels it makes great sense to fire on as many cylinders as possible and use them all. The more you do, the wider you spread the net, the greater the chance of reaching your prospects (as most people will engage through multiple channels over an extended time period before committing to buy and join) but your business will also increase its chances of getting noticed by the search engine algorithms.

And the more times you get noticed with positive signs and trends, the more likely your business is to be found moving up the search rankings for the keyword phrases driving whatever products or services you offer.

Summary – *Don't keep your light under a bushel, whatever that is! Be excited about your business through as many online channels as practicable and don't be afraid to engage external help – the costs can be less than you'd expect and third parties can quickly learn about your business and bring new ideas to the table.*

Chapter 38
Remember You Are Unique

Don't use the same information, articles, approach and style in each channel

Again, we are harping on about this because it's such a tempting trap to fall into and eventually most businesses lose their good intentions, or new staff join without the right knowledge, and you will see the same old content being repeated through each channel.

What exactly do we mean by this?

Let's say you create a press release about a new product launch or you are attending a trade show, or your online marketing agency or PR company create something for you – naturally they will add it to the website or whatever online presence you've chosen, they may syndicate it out to their network of influencers, and they'll probably ask for it to be added into the blog and social channels.

This is a mistake. Duplicate content works for no-one but the lazy employee.

What can be done is retell the same story from a different perspective. So for example one *article* might talk mostly about all the branding decisions behind the new product, in another you might talk about the technical issues and innovations in the product itself – this will speed up the time taken to think about what you are going to talk about, but still fulfil the necessary elements of uniqueness required for the search engines and even if your prospects read everything, they won't be as upset and starting to read old thing twice!

You can of course try and reuse content on different channels but several months apart – in the hope that your audience will have forgotten they've seen it before.

But preferably only use it once.

In short, a lot of this comes down to a bit of advance scheduling both of the planned content and topics, but also what's best suited to each channel and making enough resource available to do the writing properly, not rushing it out unless it's a real genuine breaking story.

Summary *- It's the planning again!*

Chapter 39
Getting Help

I've lost count of how many times the phrase, *have you Googled that?* gets spoken in our agency, but it's no crime to do so when developing your online marketing strategy.

Obviously we say Google when we could mean any search engine but in practice with Google driving the bulk of commercial web traffic for most businesses, it makes sense to consider starting there.

We are NOT necessarily suggesting you ask Google (via Webmaster tools and its various advice for webmasters for example) how to do something as I am of the very strong opinion that:

- They won't tell you a straight answer as Google (when all else is considered) is really all about pushing a Paid-for advertising agenda, so that's not in your favour
- They can't tell you a straight answer as it's very unlikely that any single person in Google knows everything that's going on so can give a fully truthful answer, even if they wanted to. If you've ever worked in a large organisation you will perhaps appreciate the view that it's nigh on impossible to find anyone who understands a company's complete strategy, even the CEO.

In our view, independent agencies with a good cross section of clients to study can generally give a better overview of the search engine giant's strategies, so ask them for advice. It may even be free.

But what we *are* suggesting is don't be afraid of typing a question *into* Google itself and seeing what advice you get from the numerous indexed websites, not Google. You are merely using Google as the curator of information or librarian of data, not the author of it. As an example, *how long should my meta-description be* will reveal lots of varied answers from good and bad sources.

Beyond technical help on specific issues, help of another kind can also be found online. We have talked already about the need to have a site with unique content that regularly changes. This isn't always easy to achieve for every page and let's face it, some businesses are just plain boring. In this instance what you can consider doing is adding in some content from third party sites. If you imagine a scrolling news ticker you are on the right lines. This will have the advantage of adding something new to your page, it will also make the search engines (with current algorithms so this may change) feel that the inception and creation date of your page has just been updated too. That third party help may be old news but it could just help you look more modern and newsworthy to the search engines. This is also currently a safe strategy. Other ways of "borrowing" content generally won't be.

Sites like https://feedgrabbr.com/home/ are a useful source of resource. NB. You won't of course be seen as the originator of said news content, which right will go to whoever got indexed first by the search engines and or was classed as the relevant real author.

Summary – *The help's probably out there if you look for it and not everything costs money. But don't try tricks or shortcuts unless you are aware of the risks.*

Chapter 40
Your On-going Digital Marketing

In the next section *Your On-going Digital Marketing*, I am focusing on making sure that you keep up to date, ensure that you learn the latest tricks and keep abreast of all the digital tricks. As you may know from *old* marketing, this isn't a *get it right once and relax* but a continuous process.

There are many practical tips and actions that you can take to ensure you stay ahead of the game and I introduce you to some of the concepts that will stand you in good stead, now that you are up and running effectively in the digital marketing world.

You may find, for example, that you want to migrate your website or update some of the materials, and then find that your online presence has disappeared. Believe me this can happen even if you think you've got it covered. If you read the final volume, I will alert you to those dangers and even help you have a little fun on the way.

Section 5
Your On-going Digital Marketing

Chapter 41
Keep Updating

OK, so you've created your desired web presence that fits around your budget and business goals and you've implemented our advice re how best to optimise said content so you get found easily on the Internet. That must mean you're finished until it's time for a redesign, right?

Wrong with a capital W.

Sadly, Internet marketing requires constant effort for the simple reason that the search engines keep dusting off their indexes of stored information (presumably to save money as it's a huge source of cost and terribly energy inefficient to needlessly store old irrelevant data) plus of course in an effort to ensure they themselves remain fashionable they must be constantly on the search for whatever is top of the charts in news terms. This is a philosophy that therefore runs through all the big technology businesses.

There are some good and bad things you need to be aware of when it comes to the daily, or at very least, regular housekeeping of your online content.

It's good to have regularly changing content.

We have already talked about this aspect from various standpoints – in general it's a great idea to review the main pages of your website, products or other online information every three months or so and, where it's practicable to update them in some way, do so. This could include adding in a seasonal element or maybe updating a page with the latest designs, colours, prices or customer testimonials.

For pages of a more fixed nature, for example those that explain in greater detail what you do, try and rewrite the content from another angle so you can bring in fresh keywords or phrases. And please don't be tempted to also leave in all the old ones so you end up keyword stuffing the page. Just leave in the main ones.

Even if this is difficult don't be afraid to have a look at the hidden meta-data, both titles and description, and revise this by having a play with the *advert* you are putting in front of the world. You could also look at changing meta-keywords although these are less vital now than in the past as not all search engines will read or be influenced by meta-keywords (as they've been overused). In general terms though it makes sense to do something, as trends and algorithms change, yesteryears hot thing may never be hot again but luke warm could be better than nothing.

Ditto H tags (Heading) and Alt tags (Alternative Text) – so you are reviewing headings and images too.

The most modern iteration of these hidden data elements are the various Schema that are recommended by the search engines – and in all cases it won't do your business any harm to give these a spring clean from time to time as they are, more than ever, trying to deduce who you are and what you do (from the clues provided) as distinct from the past where data had to be set in stone as it was necessary to tell them what you did.

Again, as briefly touched on before, if it proves to be impossible to make any further changes, as you've done everything you could many times before and even re-run old information on a rotational basis, then fall back on the option of at least refreshing content by adding in news feeds or similar so that the inception date of the content appears newer.

Summary – *Put a date in the diary to remember to review the core bits of your online exposure and change as much as you can, but remember to stay relevant to your goals. Don't be afraid of the hidden data that applies to content and images.*

Chapter 42
Why Spring Cleaning is Better Left at Home.

It's always nice to have a spring clean isn't it? This may be so at home and from the way some marketers and webmasters throw away their old online content you'd be excused for thinking it must be a good habit for the Internet too. Sadly, it isn't.

Aside from the kind of changes we are talking about in the previous section, that is subtle tweaks to the content but not wholesale changes to the structure of content, then content changes can be a good thing. But what is a very bad thing is simply removing content for no good reason other than you are bored with it, and this even applies to products that are presumably out of stock suddenly being removed from the site.

Every bit of content online can have been saved or bookmarked by prospective users and if they type such a reference into a search engine and end up at a dead or non-existent page, it's a frustrating user experience. This puts off your prospective customer which is of course never a good thing.

Worse than that, if the prospect jumps straight back out from the bad page, which is called the Bounce, and they do it quickly, so that's the Bounce Rate, then this gets noticed by the search engines. A high bounce rate makes the search engines feel bad as they delivered a less than useful experience and more importantly than that it makes **them** look bad. This is their biggest fear, that they look bad, so we all start searching somewhere else, which is the last thing the search engine owners want. The result is they punish offending content, severely.

Even worse than that, they punish the whole website, so in effect the whole business: you make them look bad, and they make you disappear. And by disappear we do mean that they can remove your whole website from the index of data so that you really don't exist online unless a prospective customer knows and types in your exact URL into their browser. In short, you will not get found in any search engine results however deep you delve once the engines have gone beyond a reprimand into outright punishment and penalisation.

Whenever you are tempted to spring clean and remove old content or products it is vital to remember to put it into your content archive if it's an informative piece and if it's an out of stock or discontinued product either pop up the relevant page for the latest alternative version or instead take the prospect to a nicely designed search page with a friendly narrative so they are encouraged on their customer journey rather than bouncing back to the search engine.

A good rule of thumb is to never allow a 404 error page to occur.

Summary – *Remember how much effort went into creating all your content in the first place so why not be willing to build up a big archive? It won't cost a lot to store these days as hosting costs have tumbled and provided navigation is simple it needn't detract from the modern feel you want for your bright new content. And every product page that is no longer valid has potential to drive the sale of a new product or a new search, so don't waste those visitors either.*

Chapter 43
Should You Have Paid More Attention to French in School?

I studied French at school but was never great at it and I'm surely not alone? It's probably fair to conclude many of us should have paid more attention at school.

Why is this you are wondering?

Most web content is authored in English (albeit the mix is gradually changing) – this has the advantage for English speaking nations that most resources and tools to aid improvement in search positions are therefore also in English. Its therefore much harder to optimise non-English businesses as some of the tools, such as directories, simply don't exist in the first choice language.

Possibly as a consequence of this unfair proliferation of English it seems as if in most countries the public and business people have become accustomed to having to understand Basic English simply to get the best user experience, and luckily for business in the UK, they seem willing to put up with this inconvenience even though I'm sure they would prefer to use their own language.

In our experience in pretty much every country, for the top search terms, a roughly equal number of people are searching in English as search in their native tongue, and this applies even if the website they plan to visit is in their home country not in England, America, or even Australia . They often still search in English even if the website isn't in an English speaking country.

If you are selling products and services in various parts of the world it often suffices to have all your content in English and just have currency and content details bespoke to each territory, for example on a dedicated country page for each nation.

Now you can guess where this doesn't generally apply so readily. France! We're not sure why though, maybe the locals are just a bit resistant to change or hark back to the days of the French Empire!

Now oddly, whilst roughly 6x more people speak English as a first or second language than French, and at least 40% of people in France speak English, it seems to be the one country of the world where if you want to reach a local audience, you do need to write all your content in French if you possibly can, particularly if you are targeting a mostly Parisian audience.

Summary – *In general, when it comes to maintaining your online presence, and if you are tight on resources, it's probably OK to focus on English, but it's always good to recognise aspects of the local market where you can. But in France, that's probably not enough to win through. In the early days of your online experience don't get too carried away on making everything complicated and unique for every potential customer or nation, unless it's France.*

Chapter 44
It's Not Just Birds That Migrate

We pick up so many new clients due to problems encountered when they enter the weird and wonderful world of website migration, that it merits a special comment on its own.

When thinking about your business's online presence, and in particular the relationship you have with engines like Google, it is so easy to get fixated on your own business that you naturally conclude it's all about you. This couldn't be further from the truth.

Let's explain why.

In our view, the only thing on the minds of the major search engines is how **they** are perceived – in short, they only care about themselves (and their bottom line profits) and couldn't actually give a monkey's about your organisation or needs. In fact we'd go so far as to say they now regard their own reputation and profit as even more important than customer experience or the quality of the search results, which is a first.

This may seem a little odd given they all spout convincing stories about customer experience and customer journey. The reality, in our view, is actually much simpler: they are obsessed that we will get wooed away by one of their rivals.

And surprisingly given brands like Google, Yahoo and Bing are household names, there are indeed rivals in search land, some new, like www.duckduckgo.com, some less so or being re-invented like www.dogpile.com or www.Yippy.com

We think the big search engines are convinced if you get a bad experience in a search engine, and this happens time and time again, you will feel more negative about them as provider of the results than you do in the result itself, and you may switch allegiance to a new engine which equals less profits and lifetime value for them.

Search engines penalise businesses, or more accurately penalise web-pages and then whole websites, because they are concerned about their image, not just yours.

This is important when you migrate your website to something like a new platform or maybe change hosting, because if it's not handled **exactly** correctly, the engines are forced to show an error message, as, in effect, your page has disappeared. Consumers could have bookmarked the right page, so if the result is a dead link or inappropriate page with a high bounce rate, you make the engines look bad, they will generally penalise your whole online businesses by pushing you down the rankings even if you've doing nothing particularly wrong on that page.

One reason why this happens is because completing a full website migration, given that even simple sites can be many hundreds of individual pages, is very time consuming – as you need to accurately map, individually, each page to its correct new destination one URL at a time. And with a large e-commerce site of maybe 200,000 pages imagine how long that takes even using tools like Screaming Frog to partially automate things. It could take, say, the equivalent effort to 0.3 FTE employed for a whole year.

Most web developers, designers or in-house web teams are short on time (or aren't charging to justify the costs of hundreds of extra hours on a seemingly simple task) so they take a shortcut and tell the engines, via a general redirect message, that "what used to be here is somewhere over there now".

In other words, if the engines could be bothered, they could rummage around in the new destination and eventually find everything. Sadly, they won't bother, and your site will start to drop down the rankings, literally as soon as it gets indexed.

NB. You can reverse a bad migration and roll-back to your old site without damage if the engines haven't yet fully indexed everything again, so act quickly.

The correct way to do a redirect is to imagine it less like a low cost removal service (shove everything in the removal van and leave it in the lounge of the new property) and instead think of a premier removal service. In this scenario every single item would be listed, tagged and individual instructions as to its precise description in the new property, for example Study, third drawer down, on the right, noted and actioned accordingly. And that's how you do a migration – map everything carefully and put instructions on the web server as to exactly where the new page will be found. The engines will then find it and lap it up without problems.

Similar problems occur, as mentioned previously, when spring-cleaning content or removing pages – it makes the search engines look bad to show a not found page, so you need to ensure in a website migration or any major change that everything points somewhere at the very least (for dead pages), to a new search page or a customised 404 error page as distinct from the boring standard version everyone uses by default.

Do all these things next time you make any major changes to your web content and you can look forward to migration in the sun rather than fear a winter in the cold. And with a correctly implemented migration whilst it's customary to see a drop in results for a few weeks, it's normal then to see improved results as the engines lap up your new improved structure and content.

In case you are wondering how big a punishment might be? We won't name names here (will reveal all if you contact us!) but the graph below demonstrates how quickly indexed pages can be dropped by Google, even for one of the world's top websites (each grid line represents a 3 month quarterly period of time) so the graph below shows page saturation over an approx. 7 year period in total.

As you can see in total they *lost* close to a total of a quarter of a billion indexed pages (which could presumably be found via a billion or so search terms) split across a two year period – the pages were dropped in about a week but took nearly 2 years to rebuild the former presence each time. And it happened twice!

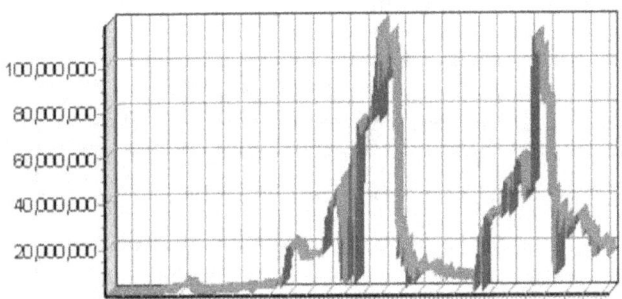

Summary – *Migration can really boost a web presence or damage it badly, often irrevocably so whilst you don't need to fear it, you do need to allocate sufficient resources. And it's vital the bosses in your organisation understand this too – not every delay is due to procrastination or a bad thing and planning a proper migration is a very good thing indeed.*

Chapter 45
Tricks are for Magicians, Not Online Entrepreneurs

As we near the end of this short book of advice, and if you've made it this far, you'll probably be disillusioned and worried, and this in turn will lead to hoping for shortcuts!

This is an urge that must be avoided at all costs – we promise you every idea you have for quicker ways of doing things, ways to automate tasks, or cut and paste this and that, has most probably already been dreamt up and tried by Internet marketers, spotted by the likes of Google, and is now built into the algorithms to detect and flag it. This means while you may gain a short term advantage, and this also applies to any of your competitors suddenly flying up the search engine results pages, it is very likely to be followed by penalisation, and may even be followed by being banned, which means you disappear and ideally need to start from scratch with a new web presence. It's really not worth the risk or hassle.

Every time you think of a time saving technique to borrow some content from elsewhere on the web or automate a way of generating content or meta, don't. Roll up your sleeves and do it properly or pay a qualified agency to help.

And every time you see a lesser competitor seemingly doing well, ignore them, turn the other cheek (and remember you may be seeing a biased result anyway as the search engines know of your areas of interest and are showing you a personalised or tailored result). Just stick to doing the right thing.

Remember that a genuine web presence is a real asset to your business and in fact has a tangible value when you come to sell – we know of several businesses that have sold for many £millions solely as a result of a strong web presence. For an entrepreneur, therefore, it's something we strongly suggest is regarded as a strategic investment for the future as distinct from say tactical advertising-based sales volume which is transitory in nature as when it's gone (the advertising budget) it's gone.

Summary – *Every time you think of a time saving technique, simply stop yourself, and this applies to both manual processes and technical ones enabled through IT systems. If you really can't stop yourself or your bosses from cheating or short cuts, do it on an entirely different business with no links, or shared phone numbers for example, to the current one.*

Chapter 46
Keep an Eye on the Numbers

To many people this is going to seem blindingly obvious, so I'll apologise in advance if it offends your sensibilities but believe me when I say, if I'd had a pound for every time this happened I'd be – well, whatever.

The point is this – it's very easy, especially with paid advertising programs, to get drawn into the excitement of seeing people click on your web presence, believe the numbers, and as a consequence, increase your investment. We implore you to, please, not act exactly like that.

First off, you need to take any web stats with a pinch of salt. They can be measuring the wrong things, for example, images downloaded (of which there could be many per page) instead of visitors, they can be double counting repeat visits, they can be downright wrong, either unintentionally, or if you believe conspiracy theories, intentionally ramped up by search engines to make things look better or charge you more. Traffic numbers can even be ramped up by competitors repeatedly clicking on your adverts – although the search engines claim to strip this out so you don't end up paying for multiple clicks from the same source, and of course if they say it, it must be true, mustn't it?

Another recurring problem is that business managers often confuse clicks for sales, so every time they get an increasing number of visitors to a website or specific page, they conclude things are going well and keep on spending or even spend more. It's vital to remember that not everyone being attributed as a click to your website will ever have seen the full page, and if they did they may not have digested it – they could have bounced off quickly.

Even amongst those that dwell a while they can be the wrong audience, automated robots, students, tyre-kickers or just people doing research.

In our agency's experience the proportion that click to actually do something the site owner intended will typically be around 20%, if you are very lucky, and of these around one tenth, so 2%, will go onto transact and become an active customer, but results often start a lot lower than this. The numbers do of course vary by sector, time of year and audience type.

But in general just because the search engines are *only* charging you £1 per click doesn't mean you are getting customers acquired for £1. The real cost may in fact be nearer to £50. A very different proposition. (£1 and 2%)

On top of this you need to allow for negatives such as complaints, customer service costs, refunds and fraud. Add back the positives such as recency and frequency of purchase which translates into a calculation for average customer lifetime value to your business. This £1 customer could be costing you £75 and only be worth £5 in transactional profit if they never come back to you again, or maybe £5,000 if they become a loyal advocate and bring family and friends to your door later. So as you can see it's vital to get into the numbers.

Remember too that any supplier, be it a search engine selling you clicks, a platform like Facebook selling you advert impressions, or even an online marketing agency, has an agenda to make a profit itself, so it's no bad thing to always question any numbers they present or where possible use freely available tracking tools as a benchmark for data that is hard to manipulate. To bring this point to life, we have seen two occasions where supposedly ethical agencies built client portals and control panels that purported to show Google's live data when in fact they were showing manipulated figures to the client's detriment, and in one case, selling the same leads to multiple clients simultaneously.

Reputation is an important guide to finding good suppliers.

From our experience we also find it hard to trust the search engines' own data which purports to be the truth. We recommend re-interrogating the data from many different angles – this often yields different results and if you select the worst performing, that is probably a safer bet.

Where search engines or other tools are predicting volumes of prospects, the various tools will rarely show consistent data and we tend to find taking **18%** or thereabouts of the highest figures is something of a magic number that crops up time and again – so use that – try multiplying the claimed figure by 18% to get a lower number which may feel intuitively right for your market. In all our tests we always get 18%, not 15%, not 25%, around 18%. Then start looking for consistency seems to fit closest to the data we see in our clients' own log files.

Summary - *Spend time getting to understand the metrics for your site and look for improving trends over say a six month period. Attention to detail is important but don't let an obsession with data take over, or you will get nothing done. Internet Marketing is fast paced and favours the quick and the brave, but not the stupid!*

Chapter 47
Be Bold, Cheeky and Have FUN

Our final bit of advice is to be bold and cheeky – as a new channel you can still get away with things online that would be seemingly impossible or frowned upon in the real word. This does not mean of course that you should flout the law, as whilst regulation is slow, it is gradually catching up in areas like Advertising Standards and Sales Promotion. In our view it is best to always try and be fair to people, treat then as you'd like to be treated, don't play hidden tricks, and then that way, even if rules change, you are less likely to have a retrospective problem.

So what do we mean by being bold and cheeky?

It could be anything – if it would be good to get a celebrity endorsing what you are doing, they are more likely to do so online.

If you'd like to enjoy the glamour of an award ceremony, why not set up your own and gain benefits from links back from prestigious companies?

Always fancied running a competition or promotion? Well now's your chance to do so and encourage more social followers.

Want to be associated with the world's mega brands? Think of something interesting about their business and mention it in yours. If you do it right they might start to follow you too through Facebook or LinkedIn.

Summary – *The gloves can really come off Online so this is your chance to think as big as possible. Just remember not to try and take shortcuts or trick people.*

Chapter 48
Overall Conclusion

If you've read this whole book and the preceding four volumes (rather than cheated and jumped to the summary of each chapter) by now you are probably understandably thinking: "Goodness me, Online Marketing seems so much palaver, I'm not so sure I want to bother."

We'd urge you to reconsider: if you get your online activities right, it really can transform your business, almost overnight. Our research suggests whichever business dominates the top positions in just Google in the UK will most likely have almost a quarter of the whole market share across all channels, and that's powerful stuff.

Fortunes can still be made online.

It just takes an organised approach and the right mental attitude as it's not an easy journey for the impatient or faint hearted, or those who can't resist cutting corners.

So let's summarise what you need to be doing to do a good job.

Firstly really think about your business, competitors, market trends, your prospective customers, and what you want to say to them. Then start to focus on the numbers to ensure you can indeed afford what you are planning for longer term. Remember that most channels will probably end up costing the same per acquisition so don't expect to find a Holy Grail, but also remember most online businesses think short-term and don't grasp lifetime value fully.

Then start to build your marketing plan and consider which channels are likely to reach the best niche audience – do think big but don't try and grab every possible lead – this should help you define if you need a traditional website or can manage with some other form of online presence of which there are many.

It's then good to look for helpers and suppliers but don't be tempted to rush into this or buy cheap – it will end up costing time, money and frustration.

It's important to take decisive action, so start testing ASAP, but remember it's also vitally important to have patience – not much happens in six months as it takes search engines this long to change behaviour trends about how they see and treat your business alone.

Make use of the free tools available to better understand what prospects are searching for, and with all data, have a healthy disregard for its accuracy. Consider multiplying by our magic 18% if numbers look surprisingly high or at the very least remember anyone selling you something could be somewhat biased, intentionally or otherwise!

Don't overlook the pitfalls of looking for savings in the wrong areas, and if you are serious about long term success online ensure you have the finance to invest properly in good suppliers, create a good name, and build a great online presence with interesting unique content that solves problems for users.

Please don't ever be tempted to seek shortcuts or copy other businesses activities online even if they appear to be doing well and tell you that's so. The grass is rarely as green as it looks. Success comes from doing the basics right, continually, and sticking with it – provided you picked the right pond to fish in the first place of course.

Even if you hate Social Media with a passion, perhaps you are in an older demographic like most entrepreneurs, then remember it's an influencer to search engines so really will impact the volume of leads you drive outside of social channels. Plan to be sociable and spread a varied but consistent message as many ways as possible, as often as possible, but ensure you are being sociable with the right types!

Remember that Online Marketing is a marathon not a sprint so expect to keep working on it forever (rather than think of it as a strip of sticking plaster), keep adding to your online presence but don't make sudden unexpected changes or removals as this will spook the search engines.

English is perfect for most markets, at least to get you started.

Finally remember to try and have fun – with Online Marketing you can try many of the things that are almost impossible in traditional channels, and this in itself could be just what's needed to make you stand out and succeed.

Chapter 49
Keeping in Touch – Free Advice If You Need It

If we can offer any help and assistance or answer queries please don't hesitate to contact us.

Similarly, if you want to make any suggestions please don't hesitate to get in touch.

Good luck.

stuart@seriouslyhelpful.co.uk

Seriously Helpful Online Marketing

Suites 14-15 Hall Farm

Sywell Aerodrome Business Park

Northants

NN6 0RG

www.sh-consulting.co.uk

Bite-Sized Business Books are designed to provide practical support and insights for professionals who are tackling an unfamiliar task either for the first time or after a gap, as well as those who want to find new ways of doing what they are familiar with. They are deliberately short, easy to read books guiding the reader through the various stages behind each business process or activity, with a clear focus on outcomes. They are firmly based on personal experience and success.

The most successful people all share an ability to focus on what really matters, keeping things simple and understandable. MBAs, metrics and methodologies have their place, but when we are faced with a new challenge most of us need quick guidance on what matters most, from people who have been there before and who can show us where to start. As Stephen Covey famously said, "The main thing is to keep the main thing, the main thing." But what exactly is the main thing?

Bite-Sized books were conceived to help answer precisely that question crisply and fast and, of course, be engaging to read, written by people who are experienced and successful in their field.

The brief? Distil the *main things* into a book that can be read by an intelligent non-expert comfortably in around 60 minutes. Make sure the book enables the reader with specific tools, ideas and plenty of examples drawn from real life and business. Be a virtual mentor.

Bite-Sized Books don't cover every eventuality, but they are written from the heart by successful people who are happy to share their experience with you and give you the benefit of their success.

We have avoided jargon – or explained it – and made few assumptions about the reader, except that they are in business, are literate and numerate, and that they can adapt and use what we suggest to suit their own, individual purposes. Whether you are working for a multi-national corporation or a start-up or something in between, the principles we introduce will hold good.

They can be read straight through at one easy sitting and then used as a support while you are working on what you need to do.

Bite-Sized Books Catalogue

Business Books

Gillian Perry
> Managing the People Side of Change
>> Ten Short Steps to Success in IT
>> Outsourcing

Saibal Sen
> Next Generation Service Management
>> An Analytics Driven Approach

Don Sharp
> Nothing Happens Until You Sell Something
>> A Personal View of Selling Techniques

Lifestyle Books

Anna Corthout
> Alive Again
>> My Journey to Recovery

Phil Davies
> Don't Worry Be Happy
>> A Personal Journey

Phil Davies
> Feel the Fear and Pack Anyway
>> Around the World in 284 Days

Phil Davies
> Feel the Fear and Pack Anyway
>> Around the World in 284 Days

Stuart Haining
> My Other Car is an Aston
>> A Practical Guide to Ownership and Other
>> Excuses to Quit Work and Start a Business

Bill Heine
> Cancer
>> Living Behind Enemy Lines Without a Map

Regina Kerschbaumer
> Yoga Coffee and a Glass of Wine
>> A Yoga Journey

Gillian Perry
>Capturing the Celestial Lights
>>A Practical Guide to Imagining the
>>Northern Lights

Arthur Worrell
>A Grandfather's Story
>>Arthur Worrell's War

Public Affairs Books

Eben Black
>Lies Lunch and Lobbying
>>PR, Public Affairs and Political Engagement
>>– A Guide

John Mair and Richard Keeble (Editors)
>Investigative Journalism Today:
>>Speaking Truth to Power

John Mair, Richard Keeble and Farrukh Dhondy (Editors)
>V.S Naipaul:
>>The legacy

Christian Wolmar
>Wolmar for London
>>Creating a Grassroots Campaign in a
>>Digital Age

Children's Books

Chris Reeve – illustrations by Mike Tingle
>The Dictionary Boy
>>A Salutary Tale

Fiction

Paul Davies

> The Ways We Live Now
>> Civil Service Corruption, Wilful Blindness,
>> Commercial Fraud and Personal Greed – A
>> Novel of Our Times

Paul Davies

> Coming To
>> A Novel of Self-Realisation